GAY MONOLOGUES AND SCENES

AND SCENES

An Anthology

GAY MONOLOGUES AND SCENES
An Anthology

Edited by Sky Gilbert

Playwrights Canada Press
Toronto • Canada

Playwrights Canada Press
The Canadian Drama Publisher
215 Spadina Avenue, Suite 230, Toronto, Ontario CANADA M5T 2C7
416-703-0013   fax 416-408-3402
orders@playwrightscanada.com • www.playwrightscanada.com

This book would be twice its cover price were it not for the support of Canadian taxpayers through the
Government of Canada Book Publishing Industry Development Programme, the Canada Council for the
Arts, the Ontario Arts Council, and the Ontario Media Development Corporation.

Front cover photo by Mina Sandiford. Cover design by JLArt.
Production editor: JLArt

Library and Archives Canada Cataloguing in Publication

Gay monologues and scenes : an anthology / edited by Sky Gilbert.

Includes index.
ISBN 978-0-88754-854-3

1. Gays--Drama. 2. Canadian drama (English)--20th century.
3. Monologues, Canadian (English) I. Gilbert, Sky

PS8309.H64G39 2007   C812'.54080353
C2007-904802-1

This book
was printed
on 100%
recycled stock.

Printed in August 2007.
Printed and bound by AGMV Marquis at Quebec, Canada.

Table of Contents

Introduction by Sky Gilbert

I want to mention a couple of things.

First, what will be immediately evident from perusing the table of contents is that this collection is neither comprehensive nor exhaustive. It is culled from writers whom I know through my association with Buddies in Bad Times Theatre, and is also the result of my making calls to artistic directors across the country and requesting their lists of gay writers. I have left out the obvious veteran Canadian stars—two gay play-wrights who are well-published and much applauded—Daniel MacIvor and Brad Fraser, to make room for those not as well-known. But I apologize to all the talented, unpublished queer folk I have missed. Hopefully the limitations of this collection will inspire other anthologists to collect gay scenes and monologues. We can always use more.

Secondly, you may notice by the way I have divided this book, that it is edited with schools in mind. Granted, some of the material is frankly sexual; this may mean the book does not serve well as a high school text (at any rate perhaps not at Christian schools in middle America). But I hope it will be appropriate at a university level, and for theatre conservatories and those actors who study privately. These selections may also prove useful to those searching for striking audition pieces. Hopefully these scenes and monologues will also, incidentally, provide pleasurable reading.

But why gay scenes and monologues? Are they, for instance, intended for gay actors? The answer is – yes AND no. (But mostly yes.) These selections will certainly be useful for gay actors (and the odd straight ones) who are blessed (like I am) with effeminacy. I went through acting school harassed by teachers who insisted on controlling what they sometimes called my "nervous" hand motions – what they more often simply referred to as my "mannerisms." What they were really concerned about was that I was effeminate. Instead of producing plays at school that would take advantage of my special talents – in other words gay plays, and/or plays that featured effeminate male characters (Restoration comedy, anyone? Coward? Wilde? *Twelfth Night?*), my teachers spent most of their time trying to get me to walk and talk more like a man. (I often wondered why they didn't categorize the masculine boys in my acting classes, who were—most of them—unconsciously doing twenty-four-hour daily, and for the most part hopelessly bad, imitations of Marlon Brando, as "mannered" instead of me.) In other words, for those men who are naturally effeminate, and would rather work from their strengths than their weaknesses, these monologues and scenes provide an opportunity for acting training.

Of course not all gay men are effeminate, and masculine men of all persuasions may be interested in stretching their acting muscles. And for those passionate about exercising their ability to experience (as actors) all aspects of the human condition, these scenes and monologues will be a welcome addition to the canon and an opportunity to move—aesthetically speaking that is—beyond the missionary position.

That's all I have to say, really.

Audition Monologues

Colin Thomas

Sex Is My Religion

"Brooch"

MARGE enters, wearing a necklace. She sits, removes the necklace, and puts it on the table.

She is now her son, JIM.

JIM   What'd she tell you?

Did she tell you how AIDS is God's punishment? How I brought it on myself? Prob'ly not. That'd be a bit too rude for company.

So with you. I wonder. Did she quote from Corinthians this time or did she lead from her strength? Did she cry? Bet she cried. Bet she came up with some really good reasons for crying. That's usually how she starts off if she doesn't know you that well. 'Cause if you know her better, see, you know she's been crying for the last thirty years and AIDS is just this really prime opportunity to pump up the volume.

It's always all about how hard it is for her.

Oh yeah. I know she loved me. And I loved her, too.

Well, there are a couple of things, I guess.

I remember once I was out in our backyard and I was screaming 'cause the only truck I had to play with didn't have any wheels. And I guess Mom musta seen me from the kitchen or something, because she came out, but—let me tell ya— she didn't look like she'd been doing the dishes. When she came out the back door it was like the light was different on her or something. She was wearing this dress that I'm sure I never saw before or since—it was sort of like mother of pearl—you know? Iridescent. And she came out and sat down beside me in the dirt. In that dress. And she said my truck didn't need wheels. That it was a flying truck.

I thought she looked like Jackie Kennedy. Only prettier. I guess you could say I was just completely in love with her.

You want to know the other thing I remember? Do you? I guess it's like my first—sexual—memory.

She used to take me into bed with her 'cause I used to wet the bed and she didn't want to change the sheets in the middle of the night. And I remember being awake—'s about six I think—I don't even know if this is real or a dream. But I remember being completely under the covers and I slid down 'til I was by my mother's ass. It was exciting, but I didn't know why. I knew about sex, but my ideas were pretty vague. But it was really hot and sweaty down there. It was scary too. And I knew I wanted to do something but I didn't know what.

So I hatched this plan. I slid out of bed and I got this brooch from her dresser. Scottish. Used to be my grandmother's brooch. And I slid back in beside her, then down under the covers. Back down there. And I got this brooch in my hand. And I pricked her flesh. Three times.

It was like being drunk and almost ready to throw up.

Maybe she didn't wake up because maybe it didn't happen.

On that day she came out and played with my truck? She didn't have on any shoes, you know. I guess it's because she didn't have any shoes to go with the dress and she didn't want to put on anything ugly. Most of the time—when she had the energy—I think she tried really, really hard to make everything perfect. And so did I. But I think she just got exhausted. And so did I.

"Eternity"

JIM   Dissolving. That's what I'm afraid of. I mean, sometimes I feel like I'm gonna go crazy. And that feels like I'm dissolving. You know… *(singing the Patsy Cline)* "I fall to pieces."

And sometimes, with this disease, I'm afraid I'm gonna start… I mean, what happens if I start to get sick and nobody wants to have sex? It'd be like starting to disappear before you're dead.

Sorry. I don't usually talk like this. I've been doing pretty good for about a year now. That kind of stuff doesn't scare me so much anymore.

Well, sometimes Christmas used to be pretty bad.

Well, 'cause I used to love it so much.

Well, it's a fag's dream, right? As far as I was concerned it was all about decorating. Me and my mom used to do the whole tree ourselves. Wouldn't let anybody else touch it. And she'd put on these—like "The Tammy Wynette Christmas Album"—and we'd sing along. She had a great voice. Sang on the radio a coupla times.

So I'd miss her then.

It's all fake anyway. Christmas.

But that's not the point. The point is…

I wanna tell you this 'cause it's the whole thing, really. On about December 21st, I'm at the beach, cruising—kind of—but really just trying to stop feeling shitty. When this kid comes up. Can't be more than about nineteen. Sweet face, but not really my type. I was into guys who looked a bit more like they were out on parole, if you know what I mean. But this kid won't take no for an answer. I even tell him I'm not really into sex, it's too late, I got work in the morning. Blah, blah, blah. But he says, fine, he'll give me a massage. And I figure: What the hell? He's warm, right?

And when we get back to my place, his mouth… tastes like the freshest fruit— like plums—you know what I mean? And he's got these eyes like—Pan or something—like he belongs in the forest, but really kind.

And I start to get down to the deed, you know—but he pushes me away, says he promised me a massage.

And he takes my clothes off very slowly. Then he's naked, too. 'S got this tattoo way down the bottom of his spine that looks like a kind of primitive symbol for eternity. Eternity and this beautiful boy's ass.

Then he covers me with these… hands. These… hands. I don't know how to say it except they were kind. And he's got one hand on my cock, and the other hand's moving around the rest of my body.

But I'm getting really nervous about something and I tell him I just don't feel like it. And he asks what's the matter and I tell him a bit about my mom and Christmas an' that. And he asks me if I love her and I tell him I hate her guts. And he says, "Try this. Try remembering a time when you loved her." And I say, "What are you, a shrink? Doogie Howser or something?" And he laughs and says, "What've you got to lose?" I don't even have to think about it and I'm back in my backyard and my mother's in that dress. He's lit candles in the room and it's like—the memory's so real I can smell it. Like she smelled real fresh. And he says, "Thank her, then leave."

And I do. I thank my mother. 'Cause in a way, she saved my life, right? Like, without her, I woulda been toast. So I thank my mother and I kiss her on the forehead. Then I leave her in the backyard. Still beautiful.

And then I'm really relaxed. And Lee—his name's Lee—keeps massaging. Sort of murmuring to me all the time, planting ideas in my head. It's like he's a shaman, you know? Like he's got magic. And then he says, "Try this." And he tells me to open my heart, to remember all the men I've fucked.

And I start to remember them. Donald. And Alex. We've all got these men, right?

And the amazing thing is this kid's holding my hand so it's like I can touch those men again for a minute. Say goodbye. You know?

And he keeps massaging. Tells me to see my father. And I do. Tells me to keep breathing. And I do.

And Lee—his name is Lee—tells me to forgive my father, and because this boy—this angel—is protecting me, I find out what it's like, for a minute, to forgive him.

He keeps massaging, then, "Hold your breath," he says. I have no idea what this is about, but I am too far gone by now to ask why, so I breathe deep, like I've been dying of thirst and he's offering water, and I clench every muscle in my body to hold that breath in. And it's like I go inside myself. Like the night sky and all the stars are inside my head and my chest and my belly. And then I'm floating in the sky, and part of it, too. Eternity flows in through the soles of my feet and out through the top of my head. And I know that my body is no more substantial than an outline, and even if that outline disappeared I'd still be here, still connected.

It's like it's all one thing right? So I don't have to be afraid of dissolving.

"Breathe out," he says. And my mind is flooded with the beautiful parts of men. Lips. Necks. Ears, beards, forearms. Beauty that's around me every day and I don't even know I know it.

Lee tells me that I am excellent at sex because my heart is open. And he tells me he thinks people die the way they have sex.

Then he wraps me up in my blankets, kisses me on the forehead. And he's gone.

I see him every now and again on the street. Give him money sometimes when he's behind on his rent. But it's not like that; he's as sweet as ever.

Like I always knew sex was… my religion. But I didn't know how to make it a good thing before.

> *JIM places his hand on his mother's necklace.*

My mother? Are you kidding? What could I tell her that I've just told you? She has no idea what I've been through. She couldn't begin to imagine.

> *JIM puts the necklace on and transforms back into MARGE.*

> *MARGE exits. The lights fade.*

Ken Brand

Benchmarks

"The Old Guy"

I'm toast
I'm dust
I'm yesterday's papers
last year's man
I'm a goddamn fossil for Christ's sake

I'm paint peeling
old money

I'm the canary that ate the cat
I'm the sight gag you didn't get

Yes. Well. So.
here's the story

I'm sitting on this park bench, minding my own you know
it's a fine day, warm for autumn
not many like this left
not many at all
and I'm determined to take it all in because winter is coming and I can't get out
much then and I have a hard time with that
I need to get out in the air
I need room to move
I always have

so I'm sitting here
like I often do
watching people
as they walk back and forth along the path
back and forth
looking straight ahead or down to the ground
missing it all, you know
the trees and the squirrels
the river running slow
kids playing tag

the sunlight

so I'm taking it all in
but minding my own, you know
I'm not some busy body
I'm not judgmental of other people
I don't care if they look up or down
left or right
still, I notice if they do or they don't

so I'm sitting and watching and
this guy comes along
sits down beside me
he's about my age
trim too
like he's taken care of himself
nice day, I say
yes, he says, very nice
that's it
we just sit there a while

then I get this odd feeling
like one of those jolts, you know
when you're sleeping and you fall and you wake up just before you hit the
ground
only I wasn't asleep
hadn't even nodded off
but I look over at this guy
wondering if he noticed anything strange
just because
well
I don't want him to think I'm senile, you know
even though I don't really care what people think of me
they can think what they like
I'm past all that stuff
still, I think about it
you know

so I look at him and he's staring right back at me
and I can't tell what he's thinking
but somehow he holds me there
with his eyes
and he's starting to look a little nuts to me
so I think I should just get up and walk away
and I know I can
there's nothing really holding me there
I've got a mind of my own after all
I'm not weak in the head

but I don't move
and then he says, you're the guy, I'm sure of it
you're the one
I've been looking for you, he says
and he's obviously real happy about this
positively glowing you might say
and I say, I don't mean to burst your balloon
it's not that I want to rain on your parade or anything
but I don't know what the hell you're talking about

then he launches into this story about how he was in another life, in an airplane
crash in another life   and this airplane was going down   it was about to
crash   but then at the last minute it didn't   but when he thought it was, when
he thought he was doomed, he grabbed this man across the aisle from him and
said all this stuff about meeting in another life   in the next life   look in my
eyes, he said to the guy, we'll know each other by our eyes

well
there's never been an airplane crash in my lifetime
that stuff's for the history books and I tell him so
as if he didn't know that already
and he asks, don't you have dreams

not about airplane crashes I don't
but he looks me in the eyes again and says,
kind of quiet like he's lost
he says, I do, all the time
and you're in them
I recognize your eyes

we were meant to be lovers, he says
you're the one
he's calm when he says it
it's obvious to me he believes it
and I'm a pretty observant guy
I can see through things you know
I know a sham and a con when I see one
and this guy and the things he's telling me

it just perks me up
that's it
no misgivings or nothing
he just perks me up
and I think, well
man my age doesn't get many offers
this guy's kind of off but he's kind of sweet too
I can overlook a lot of things when a guy's kind of sweet

we had some good years together we did
he never dreamt of airplane crashes again and that was fine with him
we never talked much about that stuff
maybe once or twice in passing
that was fine with both of us

he had beautiful big brown eyes
I'll know them if I ever see them again
I don't think I could ever forget those eyes

I'm fresh baked warm from the oven
I'm rich loamy soil
I'm the cutting edge of journalism

the name to the face
I'm the prize you bought the ticket for

"The Spiritual Fag"

I finally figured it out
why people in elevators face front and watch the numbers
it's not because they're anti-social
no, nothing like that

people in elevators face front and watch the numbers so they'll know how high
up they are if and when the cable snaps
that way, if they survive they can tell all their friends
I survived a fall in an elevator from the second floor
I survived a fall in an elevator from halfway between four and five

a few broken limbs, maybe a permanent back problem
and a great real life story to tell

the cable snapped for me at year twelve
I wanted to feel weightless
and I did
suspended
and not suspended

the cable snapped for me at year twelve
no more memorial services, vigils and funerals
no more buddy support, no more committees

the final straw came when Ray told me how he fucked over the advocacy group
for a few bucks and a free trip to New York
that was it for me
the political dyke would say I was being moralistic and judgmental about it
but it wasn't the ethical stuff that bothered me

and it's not like he broke the bank

for Ray it was a survival tactic
a way to prolong his life a bit
get some of his dignity back
can't fault a guy for that but
I just couldn't watch that stuff play itself out anymore

so I decided to hit the road
left a note for my lover
dropped Ray off at the hospital
and walked

and I closed my eyes

and there was a wind
cool but not cold
like spring
I kept my eyes closed for some time
but I could still see everything
so I closed the eyes of my eyes
to feel the cool motion wash over me
you couldn't really call it air
just something moving

and I was in a boat
on a slow moving river
and there was this man
steering the boat
as we glided along
its broken surface
he was a handsome man
kind and generous and calm
you could tell by his smile
and the river was old
it was slow moving
slow winding
at times it felt like it was winding right back
in on itself
and the trees that grew beside the river
were old too
but strong
they stretched out years
over that river
and I could reach up and touch
with no effort
some of those branches

I could reach up with no effort
and pluck a leaf
and inspect its veins and I thought
when was the last time I reflected on how
a leaf looks
when was the last time I thought about
the structure of a leaf
the age of trees
when was the last time
I carried a stone in my pocket
just because
I liked how it felt
its slight weight
its smooth edges

I touched the water
and noticed for the first
time the complete absence
of noise

I'd almost forgotten about him
when the man spoke
and he said to me
I can tell you where we're going
and you can tell me where we've been
and he said
you can leave
or you can stay
there are no right answers

and I opened my eyes
and he was gone
everything
river trees boat
gone

now
I'm headed south
none of that go west new frontier shit for me
west is suicide
and east
east is a fucking eyesore
the old world
north is cold and I want to be warm
so south it is

I was once a mover and a shaker
I got things done
but you can't sustain that forever
something has to give
and if you think you can keep it up forever
for as long as it takes
you're fucked
and you just wind up getting in the way

Michael Lewis MacLennan

Beat the Sunset

"Sacha"

SACHA   Before we close our first class, I want you to imagine that there is an epidemic in which a disease rapidly weakens the body and shuts down the immune system. This enables other diseases to invade the body. You lie there feverish, soaked in sweat and dying of some combination of diseases specific only to you, preying on your weakened body and soon, killing you.

And this disease seems to have... preferences... about who it infects and kills.

And imagine that the people who die most are pregnant women and children. Pregnant women lose any immunity to the disease. And it takes children five years to develop the antibodies to have a fighting chance against the disease.

And imagine that when it hits men, the fevers reach 104 degrees, temperatures at which sperm cooks. So if you survive, you're probably infertile.

So you have this disease where it's harder and harder for men and women to conceive children in the first place. Then, if the disease doesn't knock off the wife and her fetus, it's likely to press the little one into the ground before he or she is five years old. Makes it hard to have a family. Makes you think – wow, that's some intelligent disease, it sure knows what it's doing.

And if you followed human nature,
if you were a God-fearing type,
you just might think, hey,
this is God's wrath we're seeing,
and it's wrath against heterosexuals.
It's wrath against traditional family values.
It's a sure sign.

The thing is, this disease exists. It has wreaked havoc for all recorded time, on every continent. This isn't a fable. Know what it is? Malaria.

Malaria has killed half of the men and women and children that have ever died on this planet. Fifty percent of all deaths, ever, have been caused by malaria. And now, every year, it takes residence in the bodies of nearly six hundred million people, burying one million—almost the population of Vancouver— one million African infants each year.

All this from the plasmodium parasite,
the smallest animal on earth.

"Adam"

Lights up on ADAM alone, sitting up on the bed. He pulls out a make-up case which he uses to change his features into a less healthy, gaunter appearance: more pale, hollow eyes and cheeks, pasty mouth. ADAM applies the make-up as if he is accustomed to the act, as one might put her/his makeup on every morning, vanity turned on itself.

ADAM   I love good calves. Best part of a leg, I think. Many times I've followed a good set of tanned, smooth calves in shorts and low socks, ten blocks out of my way. Didn't matter if I was on foot or on my bike…. Bicycle couriers – they are consistently the best, even wearing those longjohns under their shorts in the winter, in rain; you can still see those bulbs of muscle underneath, pumping down, waiting for spring, to bud out.

And what's wrong with seeking a little beauty in the middle of the grotesque, flabby cities I've lived in? What's wrong with pursuing a few knots of beauty on firm legs, lurking ten paces behind them? They fortified me. As I rode or walked back to my own route, they fortified me, kept me going. Kept me sure of the track I was on.

There are things my body has lost. There's always muck on my lips, on my tongue. I brush my tongue raw, but the yeast waits in the cracks and in a few hours, it's covered everything again. It's a stupid battle. Who'd want to kiss these lips?

ADAM places calamine lotion on his chest – blotches to suggest shingles, blisters.

I was never that big. People used to warn me about catching some tropical disease, that I couldn't handle the weight loss. But I'm okay. It's just this neck. *(holding it)* I really loved the simple material of my neck – lean, firm, nothing wasted. It mocks me now, every time I look in the mirror. Thin enough? Thin enough? Like some erogenous zone gone bad, gone to seed, all thinning out.

My hair is thinning too, like mad. And the worst dandruff embarrasses me. My body is leaving me via my head. Scales and hairs. My beautiful hair.

I used to have great calves. Worked so hard to get them, too. And you know what? They were the first thing to go.

The Shooting Stage

"Elliot"

ELLIOT stands in a walk-in closet among racks of his dear mother's clothes, wearing a feather boa.

ELLIOT   "Ladies and Gentleman, I give you, the world expert on the come-back sensation of the animal kingdom, heeeeeerrrrre's Elliot!" Thank you, thank you, thank you. Now I'm sure you're all wondering why I'm standing here wrapped in a feather boa. Well, I'll tell you: it's in honour of my favourite creature of the sky, who just so happens to be the topic of my biology assignment. Yes, ladies and gentlemen, the trumpeter swan. With a snow-white body and ebony beak, trumpeters have a deep, penetrating honk that warns…"

Snickering can be heard from the other boys. ELLIOT pulls his hands out of boa "wings" to reveal that he holds a pen and file cards.

…cut "penetrating" are you crazy? They'll laugh me out of the classroom. Heathens. Let's just say a loud honk. *(returning to the speech)* "…a *loud* honk that warns it will fight any encroacher."

"But catch a swan and it goes limp in your hands." *(crosses out, chuckling)* Limp. Oh I don't think *that'll* fly. *(revising speech)* "Swans know when to give up."

"Trumpeters were killed for their feathers, used for quills, feather boas, powder puffs, and other fashionable items." *(revising)* Yes. Fashionable items, that's good.

(speech) "But then. In 1933 they looked around and the partay was o-ver! They figured only thirty trumpeter swans were left. They'd practically cleared the place. So what they did was, they made the swan an endangered species and preserved precious mating—"

(revising) Mating. Hm, no – precious *nesting* grounds. Don't give those maniacs an inch.

(speech) "Now, there are over 8,000 trumpeters. Last summer a swan stayed *here*, alone. They don't know why, but nature is returning, healing herself. Nobody remembers a trumpeter swan ever coming back here before. This year the swan may come back, and I personally am on the lookout for her."

(Lights shift as ELLIOT returns to his intensely imaginative world.) Because when she flies overhead I can see her. I can see…

The bird, bird of fearless solitude, killed for your feathers, your beauty sacrificed, fly back. Fly back to me. Your blood runs like mine. And your cry, your call to me is a secret, an old code, a memory.

"Malcolm"

MALCOLM   I'm at this video arcade downtown, few months back. God knows why. Couldn't handle the house. There's this kid with his back to me, scrawny, lean strips of muscle under his thin t-shirt. He's still growing, small sleeves tight under his armpits. He sways and jabs in front of the screen. I'm beside him when the game finishes, give him another coin. This time he loses almost right away. I ask if he wants ice cream and his eyes narrow. Sure, he says. Sure. Dairy Queen, I buy him what he wants and watch him eat it, his skinny arms encircle the dish like a fortress. When he's done I take him to the park. I unzip his pants and kneel before him, encircle him with my mouth. He gasps, astonished, his soft skin has never been touched by anyone, and for a moment I'm almost happy. His legs wobble like he's going to faint and so I prop him against the tree, wrap my arms around his shaking thighs and thrust him into my face. Inhale the beauty of this unkempt perfection, the smell of youth turning.

He comes quickly. I stand up, taller than him again. He sneers at me, probably just nervous, trying to be brave. But hey, it's this look he's giving me, his eyes, they.... How DARE you SNEER at me, EH? EH? You little PUNK! And I grab his flimsy arm, his mocking eyes are desperate now, and I deliver a blow to his soft belly, send him bent over now. I strike that body maybe five times, he's on the ground, and that's it, enough is enough. Sobbing silent into the dirt. I throw him fifty dollars. The red bill lands next to his face. His breath ruffles an edge. He's not looking at me now.

Next morning, I've forgotten. Go out there, into the day like nothing happened. Other people, they don't see what I've done. They don't know. And I start to think, "It wasn't that bad, nothing really happened… nothing really happened."

Week later, I'm back at the arcade. When he sees me, he just takes his hands from the game and turns to me, lets his rented hero explode on the screen behind him. He holds out his hand, and I press the token, hard enough to leave a circle over the lines on his palm. He came back. He came back again. To me.

Leaning Over Railings

JASON   Four-thirty, still heat of the day, and where am I? The sauna. The men's sauna. I'm weak after the island but I decide to sweat it out even longer before dressing for cocktails. I don't know why; to push things a little, I guess. It's a dark little room, one feeble light. And sitting under it is guess who, the cruise ship band's percussionist, reading. He is naked, his thick penis limp, the tip just touching the bench his legs are up on.

I sit at the opposite corner, and look at him, smiling silent… *hello, hello…* he won't look at me; he is reading. I just keep my head in my hands, catch my breath, catch the sweat that has begun to form on my forehead.

I don't look up. He doesn't look up.

How long has he been in here? And why would you want to read in this small dark room, dripping onto your pages, wrinkling and spotting them with your sweat.

"Hot." I say. Oh, good start.

"Yeah." And he sounds very sexy. Hoarse, which is probably just from the dry air. But what exactly are we saying… is there any meaning here? Does this *mean* anything?

I shift my back into the corner, the hot wood stinging my skin, and sit staring at him across the bench, urging him telepathically to look up, to see me, take me into his warm drummer's arms. *Holding still, holding still….* He turns a page and sighs. I wilt into my hands and watch sweat pool in the crook of my elbow.

And when I look up, he's absolutely still; I can tell even his eyes are resting on the same word. Everything has stopped in that room except one thing: that tip and all behind it slowly fills up and arcs hard into his flat belly. Oh. He still doesn't look at me, and I sit shamelessly watching his flesh grow rigid. He turns to face the wall, to stare at a knot, and he opens his legs at the knees, offering.

When I lick his stomach, I taste slippery desire, a scent like hot buttered cabbage. He takes my skull into his hands and massages my wet hair, brings me down onto him. I inhale him, devour the part that is him. I am creating pleasure; I finally exist on this ship. He moans and whispers words like promises to me. "Yes, yes, yes…"

This is it, I've found someone. For once I'll have no secrets, and someone beautiful will call "Jason," of all things and will desire, desire me as I desire him. For four days, at least… I've found it, I've found it…

And with the hot bolts knocking the back of my throat, I think, *no, I'm going to, I'm going to…* and I do. And in the shudder of a gulp, in his final shudder into me, he reaches, *no*, to touch me, barely. Barely. *No.* I am small, drawn close up under him. Just a hug would've…

"That was great," he said. A slight drawl, I think.
His fingers stumbled over my shoulders and I tried to look into his eyes, to meet him there. Okay, fine. Then to remember his face.

He did give me a kiss. Our salts mingled and then mutely slipped past one another, a tongueless kiss. He slowly hoisted himself up from the bench.
He said, "Thanks – see you?"
An invitation, or a dismissal…. "Sure."

The door's spring bounced twice. I could catch glimpses of him through the small smeared window, slowly dressing. He didn't even shower. My tongue plied my acrid mouth, parched and empty. Then I stopped looking. Holding still, holding still… I was dry inside, sweating clear in a dark wooden box.

Gavin Crawford

Chet Sings at the Grand Ol' Opry

CHET a young country star, enters in jeans and a cowboy hat, he has a guitar.

Hell, Sweet Jesus, I caint even b'lieve this. Here I am at the God Damned Grand Ol' Opry! This is a real trip you know I been dreamin' of this ever since I's just a littlun settin' down in my daddy's basement in my little cowboy hat and my mama's perls lestnin' to that old country radio. You know I reckon I learned all I ever knowed from country radio. Course I had great teachers – Loretta Lynn, Hank Williams, Ms. Dolly. Yeah they taught me that a woman oughta stick by her man no matter how hard he hits, and that it's okay to kill there're someone messing wit'cher wife, and also I spose I learnt that pretinear everone goes through the death of a dog at one time or another. But most of all I learnt ya gotta write what you know and I guess it works else how come I got the Number One single on the country charts right now? Yee Haa!…

You know I've been travelling around a spell touring the country singin my songs 'n I gotta tell ya it gets pretty wild sometimes. People screamin and throwing their underpants up on stage atchya. Most the time I'm thinking hell it's just me no need to get so excited!

But it's all right I guess people wantin ya to sign pitchures o yourself, course now they got naked pitchures of me on the internet I seen one t'other day 'n I had a big ol dangler down t'about my knees! I'm thinkin hell that ain't mine but it's sure flatterin. Well I reckon I best sing it for ya since that's what you're waiting for, here's a little song I wrote, it goes a little something like this…

Oh it's hard to be a homo here in Dallas,
Where the men are men from hats down to their boots.
No they don't like havin their masculinity challenged,
No sir Texas ain't a kindly place fer fruits.

You see my momma said she'd cut off my allowance,
'Less I changed my ways and walked a straighter line.
So I thought up this cover to convince my homophobic
mother that I'm not gay I'm just bidin my time.

(chorus) 'N I told her all my women left me
so I started datin Men!
    I may as well raise a rooster

if I just can't keep a hen.

    Well I don't know that it's forever but it does me fine for now,
and mother it sure as hell beats messin with
my daddy's fav'rite cow.

Well last night I went to have a beer at Jackson's,
I was checkin out some coboy's Levi-ed rear,
I said hey buddy are you looking for some action?
Then he whirled around and grabbed me by the ear.

He said "What are ya son some kind of fuckin homo?"
Then he waved his hand and called his buddies round.
I thought for sure that I was dead
But I kept a real cool head n' said
"Now listen Boys afore ya knock me down...

'N I told them

    Chorus.

Well now the big guy kinda stared at me in wonder,
As I waited for his friends to black my eyes.
But they didn't start in poundin' me asunder,
And what happened next sure came as a surprise.

You see one by one them cowboys started talking,
'Bout how their wives 'n girlfriends left them high and dry.
They said, "It used to make us tense but son what you just said makes perfect sense,"
So we all went back to my place for a sexual Org-I!

'N we were singing

    Chorus.

Jayson Goes Dancing

    Music in.

JAYSON   *(dancing)* Whooo! Whooo! Heloo!

    Music fade out.

Okay can I just ask you like what is with this place tonight. Like who still decorates with streamers? Okay like did you see that cute guy I was talking to over by tha bar ohmygod he is so dumb, he actually told me he thinks I look like Sporty Spice!? Cha hello I'm so not even British! Then when I told him my name was Jayson – With a "Y" he's like "oh you mean like Jasony." Oh yeah, put the dick back in your mouth honey because talking is like not your strong thing that you are even very good at…

I swear to God sometimes I think I have a mental sufficiency, like you know S-U as opposed to D-E. 'Cuz I like don't understand half the losers in here. Like not that I think I'm so much better just maybe a bit smarter… like I'm on a different mental plane. You know like here's my plane up here and here's them still on the runway. But it's probably good to have different planes because if we were all on the same mental plane how crowded would that be? Worse than Canada 3000 I bet!…

> *Music in.*

Oh YES. How much do I love this song.

> *He dances. Music fade out.*

Okay did you see that guy I was just dancing with, well not really with but sort of by…. Like he's all dressed up and like really cute like blonde curls and a really nice face and like actually quite Her-cu-lean? Yeah! Well he was like looking at me like right in my eyes and all of a sudden I realized hey I know this guy and do you know why I know him? Because back home in Sarnia I used to babysit him. And that kind of creeps me out because I know he wanted to go home with me but I used to change that guy's diapers and can I just tell you that guy is totally not hung! It's true…. So I like asked him hey how did you even get past the bouncer and he's like there was no bouncer. And I just said well lucky for you 'cuz if you are nineteen than I am thirty. *(pauses stunned)*

> *Music in.*

Holy retro, I love this song…

> *He dances.*

Stare stare like a bear! Seriously sometimes I wish I was ugly so I could dance in peace! Uh of course all the old men are staring…. That drag queen looks like my Granma!

> *Music fade out.*

Hey I was like just dancing with this real Daddy-type guy and I was thinking wow this guy looks just like my uncle Stan. And then he's like looking at me and he goes "Jayson are you okay?" and I'm all "Hey. You ARE my uncle Stan! What are you doing in a gay bar?!" And then over his shoulder I swear I saw my mother like mouthing at me like Whoah – whoah – whaowwaww, and then someone tapped me and oh my God it was like my actual father? So I just lose it and I go

"HEY Family. You have to stop following me around. Like I am GAY OKAY! Well actually I'm bisexual because I don't believe in labels. Like you can be here if you want but there is no way you are gonna drag me outta this club!

And then my Aunt Betty handed me a piece of cake – and all of a sudden I realized. I'm not at a bar, I'm at my cousin Barry's wedding. In Sarnia.

Music in – something wedding-y.

He pauses and looks around then down at his attire, he takes a bite of cake, slowly slinks off.

Jordan Patterson

Waiting for the Donald to Call, or Oprah, or Margaret Cho!

"The Pitch"

IT'S YOUR LUCKY DAY!

Oprah found a genie in a bottle…
But the genie wants to grant YOU one wish!
WHAT IS IT?

Now think carefully! This is a once in a lifetime opportunity, so
you need to think big. Everyone wants fame, and fortune… but
that's too boring! We are looking to make your WILDEST dreams come
true! That one thing that you've always wanted to do or buy, but
could never make it happen. Our Dream Team is searching the globe
for some fun, exciting, and over-the-top dreams to fulfill.

The sky is the limit. So if you know a Super-Deserving person who
needs a genie in a bottle, we want to hear all about them!
Who are they?
What is their wish?
Why do they deserve to have it granted?

Remember, it's all about fun!

To be considered for this program, you must send us a CREATIVE and
UNIQUE videotape (or a slew of pictures) ASAP that vividly describes
and clearly explains how Oprah can make this Super-Deserving
Person's WILDEST DREAM come true.

Write or tape your contact information on the case of your
videotape, and mail it ASAP to:
The Oprah Winfrey Show
WILDEST DREAM
c/o Team LE
PO Box 917940
Chicago, IL 60661

Avoid music in the background and shooting the camera directly into
the light.
Tapes will not be returned and may be broadcast worldwide on "The

Oprah Winfrey Show" and distributed in all other markets and media worldwide.

Recipients of makeovers and giveaways are responsible for the payment of any applicable taxes.
From Oprah's website

Dear Oprah: Here is my Wildest Dream: You asked for it. See proof above!

I want to simply send you a play and for you to read it. I have been begging people to read my play and it seems like no one will. I believe that I have talent. But it sometimes feels like no one else believes me. So for my wildest dream: SIMPLY. Read my play. You will be the first. (Except for Jocelyn who will proofread it.)
If you like it, set me up with some money for a nice hotel room somewhere fancy or remote (i.e.: Aspen, Paris, that hotel where Jack Nicholson wrote "The Shining") to sit and write. With a computer free of viruses. A computer that will spell for me, and not discourage me because there are red marks all over the page because "I can't spell or put sentences together." Does anyone realize how frustrating it is to have red marks all over your paper when you are writing? I have to use spell check, for obvious reasons. When you spell something wrong it puts these big red marks across my writing. It reminds me of failing Grade 4, feeling stupid and useless. And I am not.
I have learned this because of my mother and "The Oprah Show," I am not useless and that I can write.
Oh can I bring my boyfriend on Oprah? He is absolutely beautiful and talented, and loves you. Also can I bring my mother? She needs a vacation, something good to happen in her life. She has been really depressed lately and needs something to look forward to. I think going to "The Oprah Show" would really be something for her to look forward to. Oh and maybe you could send my mom, and me, hell even my boyfriend, on a cruise or something fun. My mother has never really been able to admit that she loves "The Oprah Show." But she has always wanted to go on a cruise.

"The Pitch 3"

JORDAN   Okay, Mr. Trump do I have a proposal for you. What you have obviously figured out over the last few years with the success of "The Apprentice" is how much money can be made by reality TV. But isn't the question on everybody's mind is what are we going to do next? I have a brilliant idea for you. My idea is to now turn reality television into something amazing for the world. I think the next step for "The Apprentice" is to move in a

direction for the future of America. And what better way to show the world
the intelligence of a teenager, than the competition of taking on Ivy League
graduates for PURE BUSINESS IDEAS AND FOR THE DIRECTION OF
THEIR WORLD. I believe that if you took a bunch of bright children from
across America at the Grade 8 level they could probably beat the bunch of
people on the cast of "The Apprentice" right now. What a brilliant idea for
you to set up a huge new show where the kids of America have the opportunity
to take on the people who are supposed to be running the American business
world. I believe that kids could come up with amazing ideas and could
effectively complete the tasks that are being assigned right now on your show.
What better than to show America that there is a future? I am not really a child
advocate so to speak but watching the core of your show, we as adults all think
we have brilliant way to outwit your contestant: Has anyone listened to a Grade
8 idea thoroughly??? They have the basics for an education. Basic means of
reason and logic. All the faculties that we as adults have but not yet completely
jaded by politics and war, and plain stupidity that America and The World
displays on a daily basis. So here is my pitch: Teachers across America pick
a team of Grade 8's that will change the world with their skills. Before
corruption of Business happens, sexual relationships interfere with the business
brain. We have a pure brain with enough resources to make world-changing
decisions. You could start a Scholarship for the Grade 8 teams for future ideas
and goals they have (i.e.: college of their choice or money for an amazing
business idea.) Or just plain old cash (your choice). I also believe the true future
of reality TV should start going to charity and what a better way for you to
make a huge difference in the world. You have made a whackload of cash and
what a way to inspire huge donations to a charity than someone like yourself.
And just to let yah know how much of an ass kisser I can be, I am Canadian
and can't stand American politics but I pitch with the heart of an American.

Just to prove quickly that I am not some wacko like Omarosa (but we named
our cat after her). I am a 40-year-old waiter/writer with tons of great ideas, a
crapload of talent and humour. I am looking for a Big Old Sugar Daddy. Just
kidding. I loved Milan on the cover of Vogue, she is beautiful. Congratulations!
Also I have been sitting on great ideas for 20 years and have been too afraid to
tell one of my great ideas to another great mind so here is my letter. Enjoy the
read or give me a phone call. 778-388-2590. I sat down tonight to tune into a
reality television show and came up with a brilliant idea. Let me tell you about
my dream with you and Oprah when we talk in person!!! I have not even proofread this letter because my computer has a virus for God's sake. I will forward it
to another friend just so I got proof that I was passionate enough to write this
letter. I will also pick this as my favourite letter to date! No spell check. Fuck it!

Wrote yah. Talk to you soon.

Blair Francey

Positive Frame of Mind

1981. JUSTIN opens his journal.

JUSTIN   Fourteen. First fuck at fourteen. I started early. I was walking through the park. Innocent little me on my way home from my friend's place. It was late… well late like eleven or so. Mom always warned me about it. "It's dangerous," she said. There was something, I dunno, cool, mysterious about the place. I was drawn to it. I realized why that night.

It's late.

There was this guy walking towards me, looking right at me. The only light comes from a few street lamps lining the path. But I know… I can feel this guy staring at me. He's looking right into my eyes. He's reaching in and grabbing onto me from the inside. And I mean he was still a good twenty feet away. I had fuckin' butterflies in my stomach. By the time he was in front of me, I was following him with my hard on. He didn't have to say anything because he already had me from inside. We ducked out of sight into the bushes… we became shadows… we weren't human anymore. There was electricity in the air that ignited—I dunno—but it ignited something way fuckin' down in me. We didn't say a word. Nothing. We didn't have to. We spoke through touching and moaning. This guy had it down to a science. He knew exactly what he was doing. With two flips of his wrists, my button and fly were undone. He went down on me before I realized what was happening. He wrapped his soft, silky lips around my cock and I mean… FUCK! That was BRILLIANT! I had never experienced the pleasure of another man before, but let me assure you, this was *quite* the introduction. There we were in the middle of this park, it's dark, and all I can hear is his moaning and my moaning creating a harmonious symphony of sexual gratification. There were shivers of electricity jumping up and down all over my skin. I was flying so fuckin' high that night and was so fuckin' excited that I blew my load with a loud cry of ecstasy. I didn't know what hit me. He wasn't done though. You'd think the guy would give me a second to recover. Oh no. Next thing I know, I'm on my stomach and he's getting ready to show me what it's like to have a man inside of me. He plowed in and off he went. Sure. Yeah, it was painful… I mean, c'mon. It's my first fuck. What do you expect? But I gave in and eventually learned to love it. Mom always said I was a quick learner. Our grunting and moaning came to a crescendo when he came inside of me.

I was filled with his love.

I've never felt so full of life.

Before he left, the only thing he said to me was, "You're a good fuck." A good fuck. *(pause)* I, this fourteen-year-old kid, was a good fuck. How many other guys had he fucked and I was good. Me. Well didn't that just boost my ego! He left before I could say anything… my pants around my ankles, left in this neverneverland of pure, raw energy. Time stood still, I shit you not. I could've been there forever for all I know.

That was just the beginning.

I went back, again and again after that, whenever I could. I wanted to find him. I wanted to have him again. Never did. Met a lot of other guys and they were all great. But never my first… never had the first again.

> *He flips a few pages.*

There was an article in the paper last week that caught my eye.

Apparently there's this new disease or something called GRID. "Gay-Related Immune Deficiency." "Gay-Related." What's all that about? They're not entirely sure how you get it or anything. Too much sex? Population control? Who knows. Who cares. It's not something I want to worry about right now. Not now. Not in my prime. I've got too many parties to go to, too many men to fuck. I have a *life* ahead of me! Okay? They can try and scare me… but it's not going to happen. It's not. I don't buy any of this shit. It's probably some tropical disease that they're going to cure in a year.

> *He flips a few more pages.*

There were more photos in the paper today. You have to give it credit. It doesn't take much time to take over. There was a photo of this guy. I don't want to look like that. No fuckin' way do I want to look like that. I don't get grossed out easily, but this was sick! He was all skin and bones. There was no substance to him at all. None. He was a flesh-covered skeleton. But even his skin looked… prunish almost. It looked like leather. His face. His face was haunting. It was… he had these eyes. These pleading, helpless, lifeless eyes. They were so sad, so alone. Sunken in his skull, away from the protruding cheekbones and… I read the caption.

He was thirty.

I'm almost thirty.

He looked like he was eighty.

All right. I was scared by that. I'll admit. It freaked me out for a bit. I almost threw up. I couldn't believe there was some disease out there that could change your physical identity so quickly.

I threw out the paper and didn't look back.

But I'm not gonna worry. I like men and I want to fuck as many as I can. I like them too much to be scared of this thing… whatever it is. GRID. Who's ever heard of anything so ridiculous?

I'm going to the doctor's tomorrow for my results.

Night Encounter

The night was chilly down by the lake. The constant wind wove its way through my layers of clothing to lick my skin. The streetcar was nowhere in sight. Only the headlights of cars dotted the horizon of Queens Quay. Work was done. I stood alone, tired and wanting desperately to be in bed at home.

The man I'll only ever know as a stranger who walked in and rode out of my life in a short span of 15 minutes, walked silently towards me. I felt his deadpan stare directed at me as my tired gaze shifted from the non-existent streetcar on the horizon to see who my companion was. When our eyes finally met all I felt was a sudden wave of unexplained energy exchanged between the ten feet that separated our physical beings. I was hypnotized. I couldn't let my gaze go. Trapped. He wore a ball cap, Toronto sports jacket, track pants and beat-up running shoes. His hair, from what I could see, was shaved short. He stared at me and took his place against the glass shelter wall.

I smiled, weakly, and returned to watching for the streetcar to appear.

"Been here long?"
"No. About three minutes… or something…." My shaky voice trailed off, ending with a heavy sigh. My stomach churned. There was something in his voice, something about him… is he gay? Is he looking for a good time? A part of me wanted this to be true. A part of me would've gone wherever, had he asked me to. The other more sensible part lacked in substance… left somewhere behind. Perhaps he was straight and wanted a good fuck. With every thought, my stomach knotted and flipped and turned. And with every sideways look he gave me I tried desperately not to have thoughts of the two of us in the throes of hot, animal sex. He was a stranger. He was an unknown man waiting at the same stop for a streetcar as me. He only said three words. We exchanged smiles, forced, mysterious, who-are-you smiles. It became a game for me. I taunted and hoped for a reaction. The streetcar arrived. One last glance from me before we took separate seats… he returns the favour.

My hands are anything but warm and dry.
My heart, racing.

If someone asked me to describe what happened around me between boarding the streetcar and arriving at Union Station, I wouldn't know what to say. But I would be able to describe every action, every breath taken, every slight movement of my unknown companion. I so desperately wanted him to turn around and watch me.

Disembarking the streetcar, I slowed my normal walking pace and glided down the hall so he could catch up. I took my time walking up the escalator so he would be able to see where I was. I made no attempt to run for the subway that was already in the station. Finding my place on the platform, I turned to find him close behind. I watched as he looked at me, smiled that all too familiar smile and then look for his place on the platform... but keeping within surveying distance of me.

Who is he?
What does he want?
Why doesn't he come and get it?

The subway arrived. We boarded separate cars, but I made sure I could still see him – and he could still see me.
King Street.
He glances over.
The train pulls out of the station and continues northbound.
I get ready to get off at Queen – hoping he is too.
As the train pulls into the station, he looks nervous. He knows this is it, do it now or watch me disappear into the crowd on the platform.

The chime rings and the doors open. Queen Street.
I step out onto the platform, minding the gap. All plays in slow motion. I walk down the platform past his car and glance in.
The doors chime. The familiar hissing of the hydraulics pushing the doors closed.
He watches me from his metal cage on wheels as I stride by, glancing over my shoulder... never to see him again.

By this point, my head is spinning, my palms are sweaty, I feel nauseous. I want to puke. I run for my streetcar and fresh air. I need to get away. I need to regain myself. I need to know who he is...

R.M. Vaughan

M/Virus

Playwright's Note

M/Virus was written in the mid-1990s, at a time when AIDS activists began to openly question the orthodoxies of HIV treatments and science, and when many people became suspicious of the AIDS industry. The play is set in a feverish dream world where M, a mad scientist and the possible inventor of HIV, is confronted, and eventually destroyed, by a disgruntled mob comprised of a drag queen, activists, a reporter, and three singing lab rats.

The play mixes elements of Fritz Lang's classic film "M," about a child murderer hounded by vigilantes, with comic book heroics, Vincent Price-ish faggy flamboyance, French Revolutionary politics, and B movie science fiction elements – plus musical numbers! Let's just say it's an unusual play.

In the monologues reprinted here, the mad scientist M tells us about his work and reminisces lovingly about his favourite lab rats and cherished diseases.

• • •

> *M is huddled under a desk in his laboratory. He is lit by a solitary, interrogating light. He is dressed in a shabby lab coat and is barefoot. He shivers with cold and fear. He is clearly insane.*

M   Benzoate. Acetaminophine. Dexatrim. One-A-Day. Beta, beta, beta… caroteeeen. Rivotril – calms the nerves, addresses adrenaline imbalances, calms the nerves, no long-term effects, no long-term effects, most effective if taken with clock-like frequency, pay attention to details. God is in the details. Parnate, low-grade antidepressant. May cause stomach shock if ingested with the following foods: avocado, chocolate, coffee, red wine, Marmite, broad beans, bananas, shell fish, anything dark and tasty, anything you could love. Beta… beta-cara-teeeeeeeeeen. And fish oil and borage and garlic and muffins full of shit-making fibre and grapefruit and C, C, vitamin C. Builds up the immunities. Beta. Cara. Teeeeeeen. Betacaraten. Alpha, alfalfa, cleans the blood of toxins. One swipe – toxin a go-go! Beta, betacaraten, good, good for the bowels and the bones and the balls and the bum and the bits between the ears and the eyes and Oh! Just Everything!
Anti-inflammatories. This lady's not for burnin', not for the fire yet. Keeps the swelling down, down on the farm once it's seen Pareee.
The following are excellent anti-inflammatories. I use them myself. The ten best

are, I say, ten best are…
Sodium Lauryl Sulfate, Sodium Laureth Sulfate, Cocamide DEA, Quaternium, Methalparaben, Triethanolamine, Chloralsothiazoline, Methylthiabenzite, Witch Hazel—it works, it works, you'd be surprised—and Betaine, Betaine, Betaine, Betaine.
Oh, Black Betaine, blambalam, Oh Black Betaine, blambalam… blam-ba-lam.

> *The spotlight sharpens to M's face. He shrinks from the light.*

No. Don't. Don't, don't don't don't don't don't   please, please don't… don't hate me… don't hate me because I'm smart.

I keep everything in here *(touches his forehead)*, and it's clear as rain.

· · ·

> *M works at his desk, bent over a microscope. He drops fluids into vials and Petri dishes. He examines slides and giggles to himself.*

Perfect, complete. Yet, not too overdone, not too busy, too noisy, too… ostentatious. A delicate little jewel, a tiny square of lace, intricate, deceptively fragile… but solid, solid as an iron casket.

A disease can be too clever. I don't want to be accused of being coy, of tampering with fate for the fun of it. I am not an aesthete.
I am a scientist, and proud of it.
A man can be too clever, so can a disease. But not this time. Form and function, beauty and competence, speed and death. The sweetest engine in the fleet.
Once she gets into your bloodstream, this baby will purr.

She'll breed variations, like a fine fugue, a hundred tiny subsets, an outcast family tree – branches bent like thalidomide arms, finger twigs curled into rickets, nails the palest leaves, bile green.
The end of the family line! It's Dutch elm in the sap, root rot in the tendrils, a bad case of aphids.
When this baby hits you, you'll know you're hit and furthermore you'll stay hit. Damn!
Damn, damn, good God damn!

> *M is overcome. He tries to calm himself.*

Visualize. Someplace clean, someplace fresh. Visualize… white. Breath in, from the stomach, hold, count to three—in your head, not out loud, in your head— let the air out slowly. No! Don't push it out. Let it fall. Imagine a match in front of your lips and your breath only makes the flame wink, flap like an orange sail… you couldn't put it out if you tried.
Visualize. Clean, clean and white. Anything white. Linen, fresh paper, lab coats, aspirin, the walls, bunnies at Easter, rats. Yes, clean white rats.
Count the clean white rats. Twenty-five a week – that's my allowance. Count backwards, twenty-five white rats, twenty-four white rats, twenty-three white

rats… *(whispers and continues counting)*
Clean, so clean.

> *Three rats appear before M, arranged in a fan, as if part of a chorus line.*
> *M sees them and tiptoes around them.*

Number 1-7-9-2. Infected with common cold strep bacteria after three years of intensive obsessive-compulsive behaviour training. Every time she coughed, she'd wash her little paws. So cute. I designed that one for the Koreans. Slows down productivity.

Number 1-8-4-8. Marco. He was really something. A team player. We're calling it Marcoderm, in his honour. It's just a little drug you drop in a drink. Induces acute appendicitis. External Affairs took boxes and boxes of Marcoderm. The pills are white and chalky, like Rolaids. That was my idea.
It's important to have a signature style.

Oh, good old number 1-9-6-8. It's been years! Venice flu. Hong Kong flu. Moscow flu. Cairo lice. Migrant worker pre-traumatic stress anticipation syndrome: "Boss, Boss, I no workee todayee, mee plenty sickeee!" Ha Ha Ha Ha! Poor old number 1-9-6-8. She always knew when I walked into the lab. She'd put her little nose right through the grate and wiggle, wiggle, wiggle.
So soft… so soft and warm.

> *M returns to his desk, holds two corked tubes up to the light. The tubes*
> *are filled with luridly coloured liquids.*

On my right, an impossibility – an answer to an answerless question. A Zen koan. An unstoppable force collides with an unmoveable object and… well… something new happens. Something nobody ever thought of before.

On my left, a little death. An ague, a hot head, a riot in the brain.
Sure, it'll kill yah – but where's the grace, the style, the elegance people have come to expect from my work? This one is a lull, a rut, a fallow period.
Everybody has them, the greats and the unknowns.

> *M prepares to smash the tube in his left hand.*

The secret to great Art is editing!

> *M stops himself, puts the tube in his pocket.*

But don't throw anything away – you never know, it might be one for the archives, a bit of precious juvenilia. Of interest only to scholars and hardcore fans.
The secret to being a genius is – keep everything!

> *M lovingly returns the tube to his desk, lifts the right hand tube up to the*
> *light.*

Genius is… volume. Genius is knowing when to work and…
Once exposed to the air, it's harmless. Like a silly idea. It's even a little sweet.
Marzipan, Chinese almond cookies. There's a hint, a whiff, a frisson of anise.
It's exquisite.

Genius is…
First, a headache. Felt from back to front. Then, the smallest tingle at the knees
and elbows, followed by pain, true pain. The pain of a knitting needle forced
between cartilage. Urine spills out hot and orange, smelling of saffron and raw
egg.
And all over the body, a new appreciation for gravity.

> *M puts the tube in his pocket and pats his chest.*

Genius is… knowing when not to stop.

T. Berto

Four Ways 'Til Rain

"Need"

I'm with this beautiful, but tiny guy in this bar in El Paso.

Now, this is not what I was expecting in this town.

This place was hard to find, but was this really cool, old factory, all hollow in the middle but four or five storeys high.

Dance floor in the bottom and stairs up the rest.

And the place is exactly half and half between Mexican Americans and pink Northern-European Americans. And everybody's everywhere.

And there *I* am.

I don't know anybody.

Don't know either culture.

I've just been working in the burning desert, doing this bitch of a study, for two months. I'm hiking thirty K a day under the relentless sun and my hair is like white and my skin is like olives and there's not a drop of fat on me anywhere and I'm trying to put enough beers into me so I can start talking to strangers.

Nobody's being really receptive tonight, 'cause this is a club and there's sharks in the water and it's mercenary.

And then I look through this sea of all these people, all mixed up and I realize, even though they're all standing next to each other, they're actually still completely separated into cliques, posses, totally fenced in against, well, everyone else.

So I get drunk enough and I just start blabbing to this one, lone, beautiful, uh, little guy.

Maybe 28.

Perfectly formed but you know, short.

Maybe five-five.

But ya know a lot of them are short anyway, or so it seems.

Anyway I say something and he keeps looking around to see who I'm talking to.

Sort of like the opposite of DeNiro.

And I say, "Yeah, I *am* talking to you."

And he still looks around and then finally asks "why?"

And I laugh and I say "Well hey, it is a queer-bar… why do you think I'm talking to you?"

And he says "but no…" or some such and looking around as if I can't see him 'cause the lights are low or something, and he realizes I'm looking right at him. And then he says really tentative
"But you are white."
…and right away I can tell he's ashamed and awkward and wishes he hadn't said it the second he says it.

And I jump right in and say I don't give a fuck or some such and I can tell he's about to ask why, "Why am I talking to him" so I pre-empt him and tell him that I think he's very – uh I probably said "attractive" 'cause "hot" sounds so slutty – but anyway, say it like "duh, what do you think I'm talking to you for?"

'Cause you gotta be straightforward – life's too fucking short, and I know, I can tell, that this guy doesn't go home much with guys from the bar.

So he kinda cools out and I touch him, just on the neck, ya know not real intimate like the face, but still with that male camaraderie shit like touching a shoulder, and I say,
"Let's have some beers."

> *Pause.*

So we do.
And about every four minutes this doubt crosses his face about the actuality of what's transpiring.
He's a bit like a dog that's been kicked, but you're feeding him anyway.
Any fast move and his eyes flash. He's tryin' to relax but he can't.
Adrenaline battling his hormones.
So I just keep trying to get him to cool. And he does.
Sort of.
With the beer.

> *Pause.*

And then, I tell him what I'm doing, working for the university in the desert, and I see his eyes get big, and I guess I see he realizes that I'm like not working class or something – I guess maybe that's what he expected me to be?
I dunno, I mean, I'm wearing jeans – I mean I'm cleaned up… but only so far. Don't wanna send the wrong signal.

Anyway, I tell him about this, this work and then it happens.
He goes to say… this thing.
This thing *under* his breath, but just at the very moment he says it the music drops volume and I hear it as clear as a bell.

"Could you be the one?"

And I pretend I didn't hear it. And he's frozen again so I start talking some other shit.
But I know exactly what he meant.

The one out there waiting that will be, you know, not like every other person.
One that might offer that chance. For...
and you know, in a different world... that could've happened.
Him and me.
I'd like to think.
I know that feeling. That's naked fucking hope, the only thing that keeps half of us alive.

But I know that's not gonna happen. I'm never gonna see him after tonight.
I got someone that I've been meaning to dump back home, in freezing Ontario, but I'm just way too much the coward.
But that and this.
No, it's way too complicated.

It's fucking international.
But more than that.
I'm mercenary.
I'm carnivorous.
I know what I want.

So we get back to his place, and it's just *so* set up in waiting, waiting for that "one."
He's some medical professional and he's *so* looking for someone that's up to some standard.

It's beautiful and clean and baroque and... empty.

You can tell.
You could see his life.
Photos... from the military; an officer in the med-core; with his family.
The small guy, but the athletic one.
You could feel his mother's worried pride in the huge family photo.

All this raging... yet quiet, dignity.
A force in him.
Controlled movements.
Like we're doing a dance.

He's so ready for... that guy.
But it's not me.
Ready for some guy not to fuck, but to go through the ether with, kick against the pricks with, and all that.
So.
And all he wants to do is hold me. And all I want to do is fuck him.

So it moves my way.
And he still thinks I can be that guy.

And I get what I want.

Pause.

And then, *then after...* I drop the bomb.
I tell him the contract's almost up, and too bad I didn't meet him right when
I got here, and I'm flying back up north in another 12 days or so.
And I just watch him age and wither in front of my eyes.
Like I just swindled him.
And I don't mean to be cruel.
But that's what *I'd* want.
Up front, hit me and hit me hard.
Don't waste another second of my time.

Longer
Monologues

Peter Lynch

Dig the Leaves Outta Your Hair and Then Variety Store

Night – Queen's Park.

VOICEOVER   *(as Carl Bart Davies wanders through the audience singing softly)*
The Men we cannot see are everywhere. Behind trees, on benches, picnic tables milling around chastising themselves. All are of the quietly hysterical variety. Enter Carl Bart Davies. Now of the quietly hysterical set only the hysterical remain. Of Carl it can be said that he is a beast child, a Caspar Hausen of the gay scene. Toppling over this is his art fag streak, his natural performance ability, an innate desire to impress others with his lack of linear thought. Carl loves to rattle others, to shake people up, to show people themselves and their fears because fear is a travelling friend for Carl and as tireless as he is and equally as valid. He loves to walk through the parks at night singing to keep himself flying high and feeling good and comfortable. He is calling out for more humanity – human recognition. His wish is to see others and have THEM see HIM and to glean from what he puts out their own enjoyment and understanding. He is torn by serious mindedness and pure grand scale performance so in this it is not so much affectation but wholesale honesty and charm. But he sees the difference between being always on and on and on and reality. This is the source of lots of pain for him. But now he is doing his cakewalk checking out the guys looking for that 2 a.m. sister girlfriend to have a level five with. Finding nobody of that description he ends the counter-clockwise search and stands centre.

CBD   Skanked! I am skanked out! Used. Used up. In a hairshirt girdle. I was picking the stray Chinese food bits out of my mottled pube at a party before coming here to this carousel of nellies, this emporium of fags, baby bad boys, suppository Neds, Mousie shaggers, sister, monas, Mary Margaret O'Haras, skirts, nasty men, wolves, holes – holes like me. *(pause)* Well, here I am, in the dark in the park for another dig the leaves out of your hair encounter. Why *do* I come here? It's probably because I can't deal with the bars or the gay scene or maybe I'm just a slut. But now that I'm here it's even worse than that. It's some kind of macabre meat market / ghosts on parade / gay men's pictorial. I mean, look at *that* girl. *She* looks like white death on stilts and then there's *this* one – is this person *really* wearing a vermilion nylon lycra spandex jumpsuit??!! And that girl – she looks as though she's taken enough nembutals to kill everyone in this park a million times over. And then there's the police coming through intermittently. Oh well, no frantic fellatio in the front foyer for me tonight. I'll just go home, cry, dream and think of Winnie Mandela's testimony.

He almost exits, then reenters.

But then, no, somehow, inexplicably, no. It's sometimes difficult coming here. You sometimes know early in the morning that you're going to end up here, after you've dealt with morning bone by taking that unwieldy turkey and wringing its neck on the chopping block and after you've had your spiral dump with one sturdy but now dead gremlin hanging off of it then you know. As I know. I'm doing my "grand old lady of the slag heap" walk.

Song: "The Dance At The Gym: Blues" from "West Side Story" – it cuts out abruptly.

Nobody can look one another in the eye here. Everyone here just does their scathing fag routine with their ugly upper lips perched in sardonic gruesomeness. Or they pull their Aunt Clara routine. Duh, Duh, Duh, Duh. Just fuckin' everyone here is pullin' a full Aunt Clara tonight and that's just after my first perusal. It's probably not gonna get any better. I can just feel it. I was in here the other night and I was talking to this wasted piece of skin (but your dick doesn't know that about the person and even if your mind tries to inform your dick it can't compete against your dick) and I was being a gracious lady talking all topics I knew best and smiling the right way offering out my sex-a-tronic signals and my dick was moving like a cursor in a computer "metronome dick." "You talk too much." "What?" I said. "You talk too much if you didn't talk so much you could've had my dick in your mouth." And I said "Oh," then I said "Boo. Boo-hoo boo-hoo hooo hooo hooo hooooo hoooo (grotesque now) HEE HEE HEE HEE HA HA HA HA HA HA HA HA HA HA!!!!!!!" Fuck off. Oh yeah, I cried marbles over that one. Laughed my fuckin' guts out more like it. And then I said, "Look broad, you wanna suck job I'll give ya one right now. Don't worry I know how to keep my mouth shut long enough to do that. (*He leaves stage and chases man up the stairs.*) C'mon. I'll do it right fuckin' now. What ya got there anyway? I'm all lips c'mon right under this fuckin' tree! Right here! Right now!" And she pulled a full "Clara" over that and split right away. (*He saunters down stairs back to stage.*) Yes, that's right. Goodbye, get lost, fuck you, my stupid little fuckin' broad! Apparently you're not one for *bon mots*. Well, you'll get none from me. But that's what's wrong with some of the older guys (not always – it can be ones closer to my age) but they don't have any interest in the younger talkative ones. Except maybe for one thing and even then they won't give you a second look because they think about your age and think about their own age and get all fuckin' weird and almost depressed about it. I don't know don't care because I'm a "heat chick" and scouting out some angry head this eve.

Song: "Fever" – La Lupe version.

(rolling his eyes) Oh yeah, right. I wonder what the freeze frames are doing on the home shopping club tonight. Maybe there's a mongo-sized cock on the screen right now in freeze frames at a distance, closer up, right close up to be viewed at different angles. It would beat a cubic zirconia I can tell you. Last night, there was this one viperous presence with his nostrils flared and viperous steam coming out of them. His holes were all open – open wide enough to do a morality play in there, just shove a pageant wagon up inside them, hang some coloured strips of gauze and you got it. Anyway, this viper bitch was eyeing this young plump turkey dinner and I said to the kid, "Honey, you're gonna need a skin graft afterward." But he looked genuinely pleased and proud – this kid did about this gaudy love show with peni in a kind of handcuffed water ballet. That's about all we're gonna get around here tonight, I've seen nothing better. You usually get a suck job side view. A little side show, dog show with slobber and all. But not tonight. I wanna blow a joint. *(goes over stage right)* Suck down on it, fuck down on it, fuckin', suckin', doin' it all. *(He takes joint out of cigarette package.)* I should do my beauty. I could do my beauty anywhere, in a duststorm with five angry jackdaws pulling my hair out by the roots. *(He hauls about five to ten long hauls off it and then eats it.)* Oh there is comfort in the carcinogenic core. *(He crosses to stage left.)* Like when I used to do pills and it got to be too much. I'd keep a small orange in my pocket and then I'd squeeze it when I felt my hand was having a micro or more like "multigasm" – call it a cell spaz out. It kept me from going too mee mee 'cause my blood was rushing like fizzy plasma. If plasma could fizz, would it fizz for me? I *have* to do my beauty. *(He gets out of his bag a fair- to large-sized beauty bag with doo-dads and what nots. First he pull out a large bottle of rubbing alcohol.)* Rubbing alcohol – primarily for splashes that drive away those large carbuncles on the chest and back. Ugly. Ug-ly. *(He removes his shirt and splashes the rubbing alcohol on his back and chest. And this with an insane grin.)* AAAH! That heals every cavern. *(Next item.)* Rose water. For to drive away that skanky rubbing alcohol smell. Mmmm. Let the wind take that hidden kiss while I dry. Now. *(He takes out a container of baby powder.)* Sprinkle on the pastry powder, la-de-da! Now for the countenance of sexual shame and impatience. And believe me, babe. It'll take lots of covering to hide that, try a trowel! *(He takes out compact.)* My mother gave this to me. It's almost like an empty little Zeigfeld palace. *(He does his face with harsh, broad strokes.)* Powder and paint make a girl what she ain't. But what she ain't they'd like to get to know. *(He rubs and blends within an inch of its life.)* They'll eat the cake and choke on the frosting A HA! Off. *(He sprays his face and body with Off, covering his eyes.)* Oh shit, that just fucked up the rosewater! Now, some MAC lipstick for the "natch look." I don't even need to look in the mirror to do this. I'll just follow the curve of my mouth. And I'll keep that curve working all evening. *(Now frantically he starts taking out deodorant and breath savers.)* Destinkum, destinkum. *(He rolls it on.)* And some minty chill night wafer. Oh, and was I scrupulous enough? *(He takes out baby powder and sprinkles lower region.)* Carpet fresh your pube why not? Beats rinsing out your underwear or turning it inside out so that the poo side is on

the outside and then you better hope the lighting is REALLY fuckin' low in that instance… or just don't wear undies at all under your cutoffs, summer's hot enough as it is, why suffer with more doughnut grease than you have to? It settles on your inner thigh and culminates into cock cheese you open your legs to take a picture of his widening mouth and he's smack dab face to face with a slimy coral reef with several different coloured singing lobsters hanging off of it. Oh it's never happened to ME personally I clean my hole scrupulously so it can house… what I choose. I've always been like that. (*He puts stray beauty products in bag.*) Wish I'd brought my gel with me, overkill isn't even a word I ever pay any attention to. How rich, I'm ready. Cake walk!

Song: *"A Pretty Girl is Like a Melody."*

Oh what a bunch of lawn gnomes, they're all quiet and weird. Not looking or talking like there's anything to be said "Where are you coming from tonight?" "Havin' a good time tonight? Lookin' for a better one?" "Oh I was at Colby's," "I was at Woody's," "I was at my boyfriend's place." Y'know wouldn't it be great if the parks went on in broad daylight just like they did at night? Then you'd get people walking in on their lunch with their lunches in hand, checking everyone out and their Lean Cuisine. Then if you didn't like the person you could just say "Sorry, gotta get back to work." Why shouldn't people get off in the middle of their shitty day when they need it most? (*He looks behind him.*) There's a paltry posse of them pressed up wrinkled and hawklike against a cracked and aging preserve jar. They all think I'm a fuckin' freak so I'll say whatever I want about the warbling old pea hens. There's two good ol' Baby Jane dolls of that description here tonight, cross between Chatty Cathy and Mao Tse Tung. Good old turkey-ass lips and some kind of hare-lipped toucan both laughing at the few really young ones in their slut gear. Like they wouldn't look like a pair of quagmires falling off of a cupcake frill in the same outfits. The turkey-ass-lipped guy's face is like a pink, dribbly gullet. Rather like a fake vomited crest. I saw him in the daytime, he wasn't laughing then I'll tell ya. I think his face is covered in mystery bubbles. And the toucan just gawks all the time. I want a cigarette. (*takes out pack*) Shit, none left. Oh I'm a crackbaby with no heartbeat over this one. Well I know where there's an old guy sitting on a picnic table over there. (*He walks to stairs.*) Darling, do you have a stray smoke with my name on it which is Carl by the way, let's dig down deep now but don't hurt yourself unless that's the desired effect. (*pause*) Hun, do you have smoke? (*Longer pause. CARL immediately goes centre and begins the living dead interpretation of "Dance of the Sugar Plum Fairy" or some such, dancing in a figure eight.*) "If you could skate it would be great if you could skate a figure eight, that's the circle that turns round upon itself." (*He repeats the chorus two times ending with a disoriented pirouette.*) Y'all out hun? Okay, thanks for your time. (*Walking back to stage, muttering.*) Why didn't you just say so ya fuckin' weirdo before I went and did my nellie number. Oh to travel pinkishly clouded, shrouded. Oh, for a rub-a-dub rememoration of five dirty men in a tub, oh that dirty old tub. Well no smokes. And that old war atrocity won't even give me one. Oh well what can you expect from the dead or incarcerated. But then too much smoke is gross. Ever see that commercial with that girl and all her "really me" cute little trixie high school friends? They all light up and they pose it up and her face turns into CRAZY CARRIE'S face and she turns into a cigarette? Her eyes turn into stale burning coffee grounds mixed with mushroom soup her mouth into a kind of stitched-on railroad track and she resembles a human trash compactor in theory and reality. So basically she smokes a cigarette and turns into a stove element. (I think that's a little odd don't you?) I mean the only time my face goes like that is when I'm going through a chlamydia ordeal and they stick that burning hot swab up against your piss slit? Kind of like putting your piss slit on a skillet. *(with a strange bewildered expression)* I'm getting mustard-coloured streaks in my pants just thinking about it. Time for the final disappointment.

> *Song.*

Y'know I was just spit at! That hasn't happened in years. I was walking past these two "Hockey Night In Canada" morons. And they said "Ey feggit!" and spit at me. Now at hearing this I thought "These two must be from Scarborough." I thought this simply because of the fact that I heard the "i" sound (figgit) replacing the "a" sound (faggit) and figured this because downtown uses the "a" sound (faggit) while North York goes with the "u" sound (fuggit) Figgit, faggit, fuggit. Anywhere else is just mix n' match. It gets me crazy to see neanderlithic sleaze wander through MY park opening their filthy holes which have been lined with faecal matter since the dawn of ugliness. So they say this and before I know it I've said "Ya don't like feggits eh, do ya penis envy?" But they didn't respond. There's no way they couldn't have heard me. But they just walked away chuckling and muttering "Heh Heh, feggit." I've a right to be here a right to be queer with bells and lights and streamers and I'm exercising it. I've got a right to deflect it little man. Man, man? Yes well we're unsure as to whether or not that's the right title. The category sort of gets bent when you try to award blithering peni or just simple house and garden variety trash with a respectful human title. I wonder if they know just how much or what kind of asshole they've been in the daylight. Or if they know that they're being laughed at, turned away from, avoided, dreaded, written about and bit by bit persecuted and hated. I hate you. HATE YOU – And I love to show it.

> *Song: from Puccini's* Tosca. *He reenacts a violent operatic fantasy with a hockey player doll. Dismembering it to the music.*

Oh, the Ken-L-Ration gravy train's got all the ones that weren't granted a place on the gospel train. Just call it the Uglification Nation. Oh yeah, and then the guy who said I talk too much was there and tried to grab my crotch. "There's a rat trap in there if you dare to try it again," I said. And then he remembered. I guess it was the voice, the tone of voice, that bitchy tone that got him because he left the park entirely. I shouldn't have cancelled that one little bit of insurance with no other sexual sustenance. But what's the point – who needs him? I shit out bigger dongs at breakfastime. *(He sings in the style of a Big Band song.)*

I shit out bigger dongs at Breakfastime.
I shit out bigger dongs at Breakfastime.
I shit out bigger dongs at Breakfastime.
De da De da De da De da da
Bigger dongs.
I shit out bigger dongs at Breakfastime.
Bigger dongs, baby.
At Break-fast-time.
Shit out bigger dongs at Break-fast-time!

Oh don't I know it, I'm a street slut for no pay. What else am I gonna do for fun? I prefer to say simply, "I am a child of the Joe Orton glam sleaze set." Fuck 'em if they can't take a joke. Fuck 'em if they can! "I do what I do 'cause I like to do." Anthony Burgess wrote that. *(Pause. He looks straight into the audience and suddenly sees a very familiar face but one from a totally different community from the park. It also, incidentally, is another gay man.)* Oh, as I live and choke what are *you* doing here, doll and how are you? Ya doin' it up tonight? *(pause)* Oh, I sometimes do that too when I can't sleep. How was that workshop? *(pause)* Wow! Jackie Burroughs, that's great. I spoke to her once, she's got a good energy. Oh God, listen to me "good energy" I sound like an art fag. Which for me is a state of equilibrium. But then you know in "this biz" you see someone at a variety store once and you think you're old gestalt buddies. Ha-ha. *(pause)* Doll, you got a smoke? Oh I didn't realize you didn't. So well, what's up next? Another workshop? Fantastic! Oh, I'll be there hun, don't you worry. Okay babe, take it easy. Bye. *(pause)* What a tarrarragoondeay. Stepping out on his boyfriend and he's pretending to be all macro-biotic with this "I couldn't sleep. I was just out for a walk to clear my head." If I said something like that they'd all say to me, "Right Carl, taking your dick out for a walk more like it." Nobody goes out with their flesh packed into their cycling shorts with a shoe horn on a stinking hot polluted city night to clear their head. They're there to bare it more like. I'm gonna see if I can find him. If I do I'll give him a good razzing. *(pause, look)* He's gone and still I'm getting gawked at by the roasted peanut gallery. Roasted, toasted, baked on, fried out, old crusties. The toucan and fake vomit face have banded together with the silent war atrocity. They're all gabbing, babbling one-eyed old bitties. And then I saw a few Colby's "originals," ones never interviewed by Moses Znaimer but originals all the same. As I passed I heard them say "Oooh, work it!" "Negotiate the distance to your hole," I said, and then they said, "Fag!" "Queeny!" I shouted "No darlings I'm afraid that honour is all yours! Flatulent loudmouths, snarly, snarky old bitches what do you useless tits know anyway?" They're the same brand of whoring wretches that would sit or stand on the steps of the Second Cup when I was fifty pounds overweight and look and laugh and look and laugh, look and laugh and laugh and laugh and laugh. The same type of deflated rafts in their leather uglies are now at the same spots on the steps giving me the "dreamy eyed slumber" look and dragging their hooves, rolling their googly eyes and I just walk right past them. Or sometimes I give them the same hysterical hyena treatment they gave me. I never forget an unkindness. Why should I? I'm ready to send all this sexual energy into the ionisphere of What's The Point. Might as well forget it, they've probably got skiddies in their undies as long and harrowing as the zipper ride at the CNE. Yes, it's true. I display a bitterness especially when I can't get what I want. Sometimes you've got to fight back, let them know they're barking up the wrong bitch. Bring it down to their level. But I don't come here for that. I come here for humanity and in my mind the parks are no less desperate than the bars, the baths, the toilets or the stripjoints. You can get your fix quicker here sometimes than you can any place else. You can meet some nice people here. People that you'd like to see in the daylight. No one is without merit. And I... *(He lowers his eyes.)* I find you all so interesting, exciting and... I just want to... talk with you. *(pause)* Sisters are doing it for themselves, kumquats are doing it for themselves, pitbulls are doing it for themselves. Just wear a metal sleeve to pet them.

    Song.

I take it all back. There's no merit in any of them. They're just a bunch of frowsy fags, scratching and babbling around this shitty pic 'n save bin. The scaffolding holding up my haggard frame is starting to fall down, my pancake trowel is getting sludgy. Oh my bitches, nothing in this life is worth eating unless you season it with a pinch of your own shit. YOU CRAVE IT! Crave it, madam. And obviously I do. As long as you've got that wayward bit of unfinished business between your legs you always will. And what am I supposed to do with it? Be a mouse girl in a postage stamp sized dreamhouse? No I'm gonna do it up on a carousel of hungry diablos and fuck bags and call it dinner. Lick me where the good Lord split me!! Get on a Joan Jet wig, some high boots, a pole vault-length cigarette and a life's perspective that will leave the world in a state of fall out. See that girl, watch that scene. Survey the haggard horizon. Don't do anyone I wouldn't do – ha ha. See the world through your harsh bangs, dig the leaves outta your hair and then... variety store.

David Roche

David Roche Talks to You About Love

First performed November 1981 in Toronto at the Theatre Centre for Buddies in Bad Times' Rhubarb! Festival; director Bob White. Adapted into a film of same name 1983, director Jeremy Podeswa.

Note: Not all music cues noted in present text. Cues include themes from operas *Norma* and *Parsifal*, and from films "Laura" (1944) and "A Streetcar Named Desire" (1951).

· · ·

> *Fade in from dark stage. DAVID, bemused, sits on table flanked with filing cabinets, listening to the swell of orchestra before the vocal entry in "Casta Diva" from the opera* Norma.

I guess it started from the moment I met him. In a group introduction, he smiled at me specifically. In the lobby, after a famous analyst spoke on Freud. I heard his remarks; he made a joke – about Michel Foucault. I thought, how arrogant. *(shrugs)*

In time I got to know him pretty well, and that early opinion was not revised. He *was* arrogant. Charming, handsome, kind, considerate. Charm: that fatal charm. He was a real actor that way – he knew how to make himself agreeable. And how.

Well, if you really want to find out about love, I suppose I'm as good a person to talk to as anyone. I've lived and loved. Still, I don't see why anybody couldn't be interviewed on the subject. Maybe they'd be unwilling to talk. But I think everybody must have a story. I know I do.

First off, a little defining of terms. Just to know where we're at. Aawright.

A textbook definition of love would present the three kinds: Agape, Caritas and Eros. You can remember them by the Three Theresas.

First, there's Agape; the love of man for God, and vice versa, St. Therese de Lisieux, the little flower of Jesus. "Oh my Lord, I am dying to come to Thee."

Then, there's Caritas: the love of your fellow man, especially the poor or suffering. Think of Mother Theresa – sits on a dunghill in Calcutta and ministers to the dross of the earth.

But Eros, well that's the kind everybody's really interested in, so you can forget about the first two. Eros: Chemistry. Attraction. Desire. Lust! Yearning, craving, acquisition; frustration, heartbreak, disorder and early sorrow. Theresa Brewer: *(sings)* "Let me go, let me go, let me go, – lover!"

(stands) Question: What are the three things required to make an act carnal? The sinner must *(holds up a finger)* KNOW he is committing a carnal act; he must *(two fingers)* GIVE his full consent to the deed, and he *(three fingers)* MUST take off his pants!

What's that?… I knew it. Someone over there is wearing that damn perfume. Can't I go anywhere without smelling that damned Ralph Lauren perfume? I know it's Ralph Lauren, because I have a nose. I mean, I can smell anything, anywhere, before anyone else does. That's how come I knew Kent was in the room or, if it was his sweater lying around. Only, he never left anything lying around downstairs. Just in his room, and then it was because he was in a rush that morning and then it was only because he was going to put it away when he got back from teaching his course out in Scarberia. I know what *he* smelled like, 'cause I know what his shirts smelled like. They smelled like Kent. That faint or not-so-faint whiff of his own perspiration.

So I would smell him on his discarded shirts. I made a point of it whenever I went by his room. Went by his room – well look, I'm not a snoop. I don't have that pointless, vulgar curiosity that snoops have. No, I make it my business sometimes to learn more about someone who's important to me – especially if I've got it bad for them.

So, no… yes…. All right! I would go into his room. Not disturb anything. Not do anything more than just stand there, the first time, and take in the look of the place – the discreet postcards propped up on shelves, the titles of books; notice receipts from clothing stores, bank statements, that sort of thing. And yes, it's true, the first time I did… bend over—I didn't touch anything!—And put my nose over his shirt. Just to see if it bore any trace of his scent. And it did.

This all took place long ago, during the Golden Age of Communal Living. God knows I never wanted to live with the man. But we all voted on it, and what could I say? That he bugged me? That he attracted me? No. In the end I voted like everyone else, and Kent came to live with us, for good. Or for ill.

The Golden Age of Communal Living… I live alone, now.

Sad to be all alone in the world, isn't it? *(to someone in first row)* You know, don't you? Are you on your own? A great many people are. It's no piece of cake! Look! Nobody said living alone was easy.

Ahh, but Sundays are the worst, though. Many's the Sunday I've moved in a steady path from couch to tea-kettle to book and back again, all in a grimy, little ring. The dirty dishes piled up. Not even shaved. A housecoat on. Trying to find the gumption to wash out a pair of socks for the morning. You know the life. Nothing on TV and too cold for a walk. You're tired of all your friends and all their goddamn faces.

Here's what you do: Get out your papers. Go to your files and see what you've got. Get them all out there, papers, receipts; look, there's a letter someone sent, you meant to read again; now's your chance. Old report cards, diplomas, prize essays. Poems! Lovely stuff. Get it all out there. Wallow in it. Have your reverie. Now, let me tell you something. Guarantee you'll throw a good forty per cent of it away. Oh, what a relief it is! You'll feel chagrin, you'll shed a tear, but in the end, your drawers will be neater, your mind clearer, and your heart lighter with the thought of all you've given up. It's never too soon to learn to let go. Sure, what were you saving it for anyway?

So what *is* love? You hear the question often. Rhetorically, I mean. People don't really expect an answer. They'd like an answer but most people just assume it's unknowable. You might as well ask, What is Art? Big questions. But they deserve answers of some sort. I take refuge in the short answer. It can serve as a point of departure for a lengthier discussion. Of course, many are satisfied with the short answer alone. Having a bunch of ready-made definitions on hand can give you a reputation for wisdom with those people.

What is Art? Art is the concretization of experience. What is Love? Love is two things: Number one, it's knowledge; number two, acceptance. I know you, and I accept you on a deep level. I *know* you, I see into you, and I like what I see. Knowing you even as I do, I still accept you. That is love.

Now that we know what love is, let's look at its distribution and availability. In other words, who has love? And the answer is, "Not everybody." No. It's like a lottery, eh? They roll over a Plexiglas drum somewhere and pluck out a few names at random. You know, capricious. Oh, we're taught to believe that this is a democracy and that love can come to everyone, but… it isn't true. You'll learn, when you're older. Just ask me if I'm bitter!

So. Love is knowledge and acceptance; love is largely a matter of chance. But who is loved? Whom do we fall in love with? Well, it can be anybody. Anybody at all. A man falls in love with a woman, a man falls in love with another man. You can fall in love with someone who died a long time ago, someone you know only through his letters, or a woman through her portrait. You can fall in love with an individual, or a whole family.

Jean Harris fell in love with her doctor. Mildred Pierce fell in love with her daughter. Maria Callas fell in love with the oldest, ugliest, richest tycoon of them all, Aristotle Onassis. And I fell in love with Kent. The point is, it doesn't matter who you fall in love with. I mean that two ways. You can fall in love with practically anybody, even the most unlikely sort. I mean also that once you are in love with him, he doesn't matter so much, not for himself. It's your *feelings* for him that matter. You fall in love with love.

What have we learned so far?

We know what love is, and how it's distributed. We've just found out who is loved. So far we've stayed pretty much to the abstract. Now we would do well to look for a concrete example to flesh out the discussion. I can do no better than to offer myself as a walking illustration, and why not? I seem to have lived forever; the dust of centuries lies about my feet. I am preoccupied with history – my own. I've lived and loved. A life… crowded… with venereal… incident. Both near to home, where most accidents will happen, and far afield. And as Margaret Mead was so fond of saying "You can never have too much experience in the field."

So I might as well tell you a few things about myself, just so you can get a feel for the material to follow:

> *Opens a scrapbook. Children's music accompanies, and possibly a slide show.*

I was born in Montreal about thirty years ago… into a simple loving family, father Catholic, mother United Church Protestant. It was evident from an early age that I was a special child, and plans were made to nurture my sensitivity.

At about the time of the opening of the St. Lawrence Seaway, it became clear that I wished to become a dancer. (I used to copy all those Alan Lund routines on "The Juliette Show.")

There being no facilities to train boy dancers in our small community, it was decided that I should study art and drama instead. Therefore, I was placed under the tutelage of a very old man, who, every Saturday, taught me first watercolour painting, then marionettes, and finally Drama for Pre-Teens.

About the time I turned fourteen, this man approached my parents and offered to let me live with him. It was seen to be a liaison from which many benefits would accrue – not the least of which was a small monthly stipend which my parents used to round out the family income. In point of fact, it was applied directly toward the purchase of a large washing machine.

Today Monsieur Le Pedérast is dead. However, you can still go to the small community of St. Eustache-sur-le-Lac and meet my parents, and they will be very pleased to show you the washing machine. It's in excellent condition; no repairman has ever come to fix it.

The story of my origin is short and I have told it to you without embellishment or self-pity: I was sold into pederastic bondage for a Maytag.

However, life goes on. In time the pederast expired, dead of a stroke at age sixty. After seven years, I was on the sexual market once more. Tireder, older, a child prodigy facing his first comeback at age twenty-one.

Twenty-one. The whole decade of one's twenties are not an easy time to live through. You live, you love, lots of time you just make do. Earlier generations have to grow up fast, earn a living, raise a family. We had the luxury of hanging loose, and postponing decisions about what to do with the rest of our lives. And what filled that gap? Romance. Romance! That's the glorified name we give to some of our most sublime mistakes.

> *Disco music from far away.*

Come with us now to a standard gay bar. It has hell-red doors and a smoky interior. A homosexual haunt Dante would have loved. Into this twi-lit half-world come the lonely and the lusty, to soak up a few beers and cigarettes and walk what's left of their wits before their bedtime. *(grim)* Oh, it's fun, believe me.

People meet and sweet music fills the air. *(pounding disco accompanies)* Watch the eyes; this is a prime spot to pick up that most essential of cruising techniques, the quick look and away. *(demonstrates)* It's a vicious game and the action is hot and heavy. Let's eavesdrop, shall we?

Two men discuss modern music. The first listens to Philip Glass a lot. The second prefers John Cage, and adds, "This is a great year for Bela Bartok." "What?" "Bartok! Great year for Bartok!" "Bar talk!" (the other one says) "Don't tell me bar talk! I've had it with these queens and their damn faggot banter!" *(collage of bar voices)*

Come here often? / Warm for May, isn't it? Could you possibly find me attractive? I have a particular need of a stranger. / Just passing the club, going nowhere, killing time; I heard music... dance? / Let's get out of here.

You see "My Dinner with Andre"? / I seem to be out of a drink, Miss McKay! / Not up on the latest steps, but I studied ballroom and tap back home. / Don't you mean Renata Screech-o?

(Brit voices) Happy, dahling? / Perfectly. / *(Brooklyn)* You one of these talkers, or you interested in a little action? / Leif Garrett, John Travolta, Rex Smith and now Maxwell Caulfield... / Of course I generalize hugely, but life is short. / Immunological breakdown. / You're young, you're attractive, you're intelligent, you've got so much potential... / Janis Joplin, Judy Garland, and now John Belushi... / You always treat people like they were... trained seals? / I dunno... where do *you* wanna go? / You look just about my speed: you available for seduction tonight? *(tempo increases rapidly)* Interested in getting it on later? / My place or yours... / Like a guest this evening? Wanna fuck? / *(wildly)* Let's! Get out! Of here!

All eyes are upon you, as away you slip... to his apartment, house or loft, "aimed at a door that may by chance / Swing inward brightly on romance..."

> *Music out. Searches through filing cabinet.*

Jesus! What's…? *(draws out a sheaf of photocopies)* A list of people who have made me cry! This goes back quite a ways. When I think of some of these occasions! School yards. The confessional at St. Agapits. Restaurants. Ski chalets.

There's no need to embarrass the people mentioned here by reciting their names out loud. *(pause)* Father LaFamina, Bonnie McKeller, Margaret Ann Leblanc. *(pause)* Dougie Drake, Theo Boere, Stan Latendresse. Christopher Paquette. And Kent.

Here! I had copies made. For your purse. *(distributes copies to members of audience)*

How can any of us pretend to be objective on the topic of love when the whole culture is steeped in its commercialization? The output of MGM alone has put us back a millennium, at least. Not to mention literature, TV and pop music, all working overtime to provide us with a taste for larger-than-life experiences. And what picture of life do we get from these? A sadly naïve one, I'm afraid. Love is the sovereign cure for this world's ills; the be-all and end-all of modern existence. Was it not ever thus? Or was there a time when there was more to life than looking for love, falling in love, failing in love?

Yes. When dinosaurs walked the earth. However, since such a remote period falls outside the scope of tonight's talk, it might be instructive to cast our view back, say, thirty years or so, to the golden days of the nineteen-fifties…. Ever watch these movies on TV? "The Rainmaker" – "Picnic" – "The Long, Hot Summer"… Or any movie about the corrupt, steamy South: William Inge, Carson McCullers, Tennessee Williams – they're all the same show, anyway.

Suffocatin' weather. Dull home life. New stranger in town – he's tall and slim and powerful good-lookin' with a glint in his eye and a wild streak of pretty talk to draw you in and make you hear things and see things you never heard before. Acts like a catalyst on the repressed heroine.

(heroine's voice) "A person could go crazy in this heat. Say, where'd you say you from?"
(stranger's voice) "I didn't say."
"Pretty sassy for a new boy!" And he isn't long before he sizes her up, but good.

"Oh, you finished up at that school ahead of everybody else, and stayed to home a while a-helpin' your mama but you got tired of that so you took a job at the mill. To buy yourself some shoes and dresses and pretty things. And those boys at the mill ask you out on dates and you go 'cause you're lonesome. But they're dumb ole boys, only got but one thing on their mind, 'cept for one; you thought you'd marry him, planned on it, then you thought, no, you wouldn't. You're too good for him. You're too good for this town, and now all you can think is how and when am I ever gonna get outta here!"

And she says, "Who are you, anyway?" but she says it real low and they look like they're ready to kiss but not yet. Then he says, "That your Daddy's jalopy? Let's go for a joyride." When they get back her mama give her a whup upside the head for going with that tramp, that no-good.

"No, he ain't, Mama he's good and true and he talks just like a preacher. He made me *see*, Mama. I got a feelin' in me like I gotta be somebody. I wanna live before I'm dead, Mama! I WANNA LIVE !'"

Author's Message, Author's Message! They all had an axe to grind and they all came right out and said it. "We must have compassion." "Reach out and touch someone." And above all, "Don't let life pass you by."

Live: L-I-V-E. You take that word and you spell it backwards and you put it into the mouth of a snake it comes out LOVE!

Love! Ever hear this?
"You make me very proud. But you have to let me love you in my own way."
Which means? He doesn't love you!
Or this? "I don't want you to be hurt…" In other words, get ready for a whole lot of pain. *(removes two separate stacks of file folders from cabinets)*

(shows a thick stack) These are the files on men I've cared deeply for. *(a much thinner stack)* And these are the files on men who have cared deeply for *me*. Uh-hunh. No, I've not been unloved. I've had my turn on the other end of the stick. Sometimes it's my turn to be somebody else's love object. But. In no case does a name appearing in *this* file appear also in the other one. In other words, there's no need for cross-referencing. Each piece is separate. Distinct. An articulate piece of my history. If I have any satisfaction in this at all, it's in knowing that if Jackie or Andy or Bill or Pierre loved me and I didn't love them back, well, they suffered every bit as much as I did.

Accch! There's no sense trying to claim the lion's share of the hurt, is there? The point about love is this – we're all in this together. And it boils down to one single theory: It's A who loves B who loves C who loves D… who has a vibrator. And not a drop of reciprocity anywhere.

Oh, what made me fall in love with him? With Kent? The usual things. Proximity. You don't fall in love with somebody far off, you fall in love with someone who's around.

Next, good looks. He *was* easy on the eyes. Then, he has something you can admire. Look up to. You know, something, anything, on the order of "You're so great, and I'm nothing."

As I said, he moved into our communal house. Circumstances forced us to be together a lot, and he sort of grew on me. I grew accustomed to being irritated. I got used to secreting mother of pearl. An irritant. A shit-disturber, he was. "You left two cocoa mugs on the dining-room table last night. I'm disappointed in you." *I'm disappointed in you.* How can you dislike someone you want so much? Oh, it's possible. It's a paradox, but not much of a paradox. What are desire and antipathy after all, but opposite sides of the same coin? The coin of response. I give you my heart. Love and hate. You can't spend one side without spending the other.

I bent over backwards not to consult my own feelings. My friends outside the house could tell what was going on. "It's obvious you're in love with Kent. Why else would you be fighting with him all the time?" I denied it. But it was true. I loved him. Even when I knew he could only drive me crazy...

For weeks I waited, alone in bed, hearing him in the next room. I wanted desperately to call out to him: Will you sleep with me? *(a beat)* Wanna spend the night with me? Until I was sure he had really gone to sleep, until I saw that bar of light disappear from under his door, I lay there in a genuine terror, scared out of my senses of the desire I felt. It's killing. It's like being twenty-one all over again. Not this passion-over-reason stuff again! *(Quebecois accent) La-passion-avant-la-raison encore, calisse!*

I'm in love with him! Why can't he see that? Right now it's a secret, but you'd think he'd guess.

We're side-by-side on a couch. Everybody's gone to bed. In front of the TV. We're sharing a private moment. A series of private moments, but which one is the one to tell him? *(a beat)*

Soon, it's got to be before the next commercial, I can't stand the strain. But which moment? Why will this moment be any righter than the next moment? Now? *(a beat)* No. Now. *(a beat)* No! Now! "Will you sleep with me tonight?' *(a beat)* And for an answer, he kissed me.

We draw a veil over what ensued. A line of asterisks. Not out of prudishness, God knows. But all alone, I'm not sure I could do justice to that first night, when I realized how far I'd fallen. We fell upon each other, hungrily. The vision of him naked on the duvet! The glamour of his discarded blue jockey shorts. I am literally, authentically crazy for him. I don't even know him, but I want to possess him, yes! Union pure and total. Possess and penetrate, knocking at heaven's door, let me in WHEE-OO, let me in. Let me into your heart. *(a beat)* He can't be entered.

One of the times we shared a bed I told him why I found him so attractive. "Because you're darkly handsome (he was); because you're considerate (I thought he was); and because – you like me telling you all this, don't you?" He laughed his charming laugh. "Who could resist?" he said, simply. Exactly.

"You like men a lot, don't you?" I said.

"Yes," he said. "I'm afraid I do." "All kinds?" I said. "Yes," he said. "All kinds." *All kinds.* And I felt privileged to be one of them. Privileged – and so jealous. Ignobly jealous. It was one of those damn modern relationships: I'm free and you're free and we'll fall into bed when the mood strikes, I'd like to strike *you*.

When you just give love, and you don't get love, your alternatives are these: Suicide, murder and renunciation. I gave him up. Maybe homicide was justifiable, but I did the decent thing. The smart thing. I cut my losses, brought down the curtain, and went quietly insane with grief. I said, "Look, no more. Better I drop you than you dangle me." Well, no, I didn't say that. I said, "I'm gonna have to stop sleeping with you."

And he agreed! The PIG!!!

It's a mistake to think that things reach conclusions all the time. I'd like to be able to report that when the end came I threw a pot of Kraft Dinner across the room, that I set fire to his mattress, that I struck him in public. But no. Instead, just an unspoken agreement to stop acting, stop talking, stop caring. No resolution. Things just get vaguer and politer and more nebulous until finally you persuade yourself that things work out for the best, you're better off without him, no real harm done, it wasn't meant to be.

How do other people feel about it? As a matter of fact, it's fifty-fifty; they took a poll recently and asked people about falling in love, and half the people said it's wonderful, feels great, can't wait 'til next time. The other half feels just the opposite. A terrible, punishing experience that re-affirms the worst all over again.

There's no getting away from it, though, whatever your feelings are. Even when it's reciprocal, something always comes along to end love. If not death, boredom. Or not even anything so inevitable. *Bus schedules.*

> *Lights dim. A theme from* Parsifal.

I am Saint David of the long, long memory.

Because you have prayed in my name, I have powers to intercede with Saints Anthony and Jude, Patrons of Lost Objects and Lost Causes, respectively. O promise to publish for favours received.

Legions of the lost and lonely lovers, dare to approach and cry with one voice: O Saint David, Succour of the Cast-off, the Washed-up, the Hard-done-by, Look to us with piteous eyes, we victims of charm, of lies and deceit, of the easy laugh and the pretty face.

Vouchsafe us sympathy, support, a shoulder to cry on when our world falls apart. Confound our rivals, but reserve the hottest fires of hell for those we love, who, turning from us in our obsessional need, deserve our everlasting rancour.

(music out) Well, I'm going away, now. But I'll be around. I'll be everywhere. I'll be wherever you look. Wherever there's a cop beatin' up a guy – I'll be there. I'll be there in every guy who watches movies in the dark and thinks too much about what they mean. I'll be there wherever two people come together in love and one of them of them is lying. Which is most of the time.

Wherever there's a poor bastard staring at the three a.m. ceiling wondering what went wrong, I'll be there.

I'll *be* there.

> *Blackout.*

> *End.*

Drag Monologues

David Roche

Why I Am Not a Transvestite

First performed July 1982, Toronto. Subsequent performances October 1982, Kitchener, Ontario; Toronto, April 1983, Fruit Cocktail Benefit; revised and present version, 1986 Tarragon Theatre, Toronto; Edmonton Fringe, 1987.

• • •

Lights up on a man in sports jacket, pants, button-down shirt, socks and shoes. A table on which rests a dress box and a last will and testament.

At long last I am able to say a few words of my own. *(takes up will)*

The last will and testament of Bessie Wallis Warfield Spenser Simpson, later Duchess of Windsor, is a thing shrouded in mystery. I say mystery because we're not permitted to know details on the disposal of her estate. Information is hard to come by. Under French law, wills are not published. And of course royal wills – even semi-royal wills, are never disclosed.

Consider the Windsor jewels…. Early reports said that they would go to the French State. No, said British officials, the jewels will properly go to the present wife of the present Prince of Wales, the Princess Diana. Judge their shock when, this past spring, they were sold at auction and the proceeds donated to the Louis Pasteur Institute for AIDS research. For this relief, much thanks.

(replacing will) But if the Duchess of Windsor could go so far as to arrange for the liquidation of her JEWELS to benefit a certain minority, what might she not do on their behalf? Remember this was a woman who not only loved haute couture, but was often heard to murmur confidingly, within the walls of the great fashion houses, "Oh Mary, it takes a fairy to make something pretty." *(picks up box)*

This next disclosure is by way of being a scoop. You people are the first to hear of it in any great number. I have this from her lawyer in France, in the original French: "*Alors donc, par la grace de la Duchesse du…*." I'll translate.

"And so the Duchess of Windsor suffers her gowns to be handed over to the homosexuals, who should profit most from this largesse. Shoes, furs, bags, all manner of finery shall be theirs, to do with as they please, in private or in public, in sickness or in health, *per ardua ad astra, saecula saeculorum.* Amen." *(takes box, removes and displays a chic fitted woman's black suit jacket from the 1940s)*

This was Her Grace's specific bequest to the Dominion of Canada. Have you ever seen such beautiful stitches? And look at those bust darts: Nobody can be too thin or too rich – her very words! *(walks down centre)*

After making a tour of the provinces, this priceless artifact will go on permanent display at the *(gives name of currently popular, local gay bar)*, where I expect a sort of shrine will be furnished to house it in. She wore this to "21" when she lunched with the Whitneys in 1946.

Well, *(placing woman's jacket carefully on table)* we'll put this to one side and reflect on her lovely thoughtfulness.

(slipping out of sports jacket) Yet – the more I think of it the more certain I am that the Duchess was under a misapprehension. Because, contrary to popular opinion, not all homosexuals are cross-dressers. Or even drag queens.

(unbuttoning cuff and collar buttons of shirt) For instance, contrary to what you may have seen or heard, I am not a transvestite. And I'll tell you why: waxing your legs is painful.

(removing pants) Commercial creams like Neet or Nair contain caustic acids and smell something awful. Even when it's painless, shaving your body hair is a chore. Besides, I like my hairy legs. They're the one part of me that *is* hairy, and I'm proud of them. *(regards legs fondly)*

(unbuttoning shirt front, leaving one last button still fastened) Isn't it a pity that men get no chance to show off their good parts if they stick to clothes devised for their own sex? Men don't bare their shoulders, for instance. *(bares one shoulder)*

Or if they do, they take off the whole shirt. Well, is it necessary to go that far? *(removes arms from sleeves, keeping chest covered)* Don't I have any choice in the matter? *(slides shirt around torso until it is back to front, collar opened flat against chest)* Can't I expose myself selectively? And the wigs are so warm. And what am I going to do with what Jackie Curtis would refer to as "my flaw"? *(indicates crotch)* I don't want to put it away some place; I might have a use for it.

(fastening button of one cuff diagonally across back to button hole of opposite collar point) Travelling with women's wigs is a real headache. You have to buy crush-proof everything and four suitcases to carry them in. You ever see Clark Gable pack for a trip? He just tosses four shirts into a valise and keeps on talking to Vivien Leigh. The quality of women's wear is inferior.

Yes, when it comes to tailoring, material and durability, men as usual are the lucky ones. Look at my jacket—and then look at a woman's jacket—both off the rack—and you cannot compare them…. And the cost! I can't afford it, nowadays; have you seen what they're charging? In the good shops? For a casual little go-everywhere frock? They want the earth! And the upkeep – I can't afford that, either. It's all I can do to keep the wardrobe for one sex washed ironed and hung up on hangers – let alone, two. All that taffeta.

And then there are the philosophical considerations. If I dress up as a woman, I have to consider: what am I losing? If I put on pumps and a split sheath, do I have to give something up? Does the feminine permit the masculine to come out, or does it make a prison for maleness? The most successful female impersonators have always had a keen understanding of this problem. Carol Channing gave this advice to Canada's Craig Russell: "Craig dear, when you do me, remember that I am more like a Viking. Work on your male identity. I did – and it paid off."

(now proceeds to fasten button of other cuff diagonally across back to button hole of remaining collar point) And then there's politics. You cannot escape a very basic fact that in society today you lose status if you pass as a woman. Not only with the world at large, sadly enough, but with one's own peers – even among the people you would expect to support you! Whatever happened to that grand old slogan of the Seventies, "embrace your stereotypes"? Transvestites and drag seem to be a lightning rod for female rage. Well, is cross-dressing misogynistic? That would seem to depend on what the drag queen's attitude toward women is. I, for one, would not want to be put in the same league with England's Danny Larue. Those football shoulders. That smooth padded crotch. The malicious bitchery. I don't want to degrade women; I don't even want to behave like a woman. I just want to behave the way I behave – in a dress. *(button-down shirt has now become a sleeveless dress with collar making a straight-across neckline)*

Once again, it comes down to attitude. Attitude is all important. If you have it, you don't need anything else. And if you don't have it, it doesn't much matter what else you have. All that Duchess of Windsor drag won't make a bit of difference if you lack the right attitude. But if you have it, you can get by on very little.

(tugs and adjusts dress to fit at waist and shoulders) Look at the Chinese. For years they wore the same uniform to the office, to school, to the rice paddies. Men, women, children and everybody else. Some day, Westerners will evolve an all-purpose worker's uniform, too. One we'll be glad to wear – as long as we can adapt it to our own individual purpose, for a variety of occasions and attitudes.

And when that day comes, why shouldn't it turn out to be something we already have in abundant supply? – something with the classic appeal of a Greek shepherd's tunic: something serviceable with straps you can let down at the beach to avoid strap marks. *(demonstrates)*

And fantasy has a part in all of this, too. All of us have stored up so many images of the opposite sex – idealized, emblematic, enviable images. For a woman, it might be the way Gary Cooper sits backwards in a chair. *(takes sitting pose, elbows up)* Or the way Jimmy Dean carries his jacket hooked over one shoulder. *(demonstrates with own jacket)*

For a man, it might be Audrey Hepburn in "Funny Face." *(stands straight-armed, palms down)* Weren't those Edith Head gowns great? Even though we know she stole them from Givenchy. Or Marilyn Monroe in "The Seven Year Itch." *(pulls centre of neckline down low, making cuffs into high collar)* Or *(tugging dress down to bare both shoulders)* Anita Ekberg, Mamie van Doren, Dagmar.... So what if you have no chest – posture is everything!

Why feel limited to one image to express yourself? Exploit the technology that lies to hand. Eschew the expensive and the exclusive *(a glance to Windsor jacket)* – in favour of the existing. *(indicates dress)* And put behind you the finery of mistresses and queens, the days of wine and roses. Those days are past and best forgot, *sayonara.* Those days are gone—gone—Gone WITH THE WINDSORS. *(bows head as lights fade to black)*

   End.

Gavin Crawford

Lipstick Nicky

> *Music in.*

> *NICKY enters wearing lipstick, dressed in jeans and a t-shirt. He has been tinkering with a motor.*

So Uh…

> *He stops, refreshes his lipstick and then speaks.*

> *Music out.*

So yesterday I'm in the shop workin on this Volvo needs a belt tightened it's probably like a five minute ten minute job max. And I'm pokin around when this guy walks into the back, like real Joe yuppie guy eh. Jesus I wish you'd a seen this guy right 'cause I mean we are talking like total freak of nature guy eh like first off his suit eh. It's like the total wrong fabric for the season.

And secondly the colour it's like way off, eh, 'cause all you gotta do is take one look at this guy to realize the man is OBVIOUSLY a winter.

But I don't say nothin right 'cause he's a customer and you want to be nice to the customers right so I just start tellin him about his car and shit right but the guy's like lookin at me real funny like I got somethin on my face eh so's I ask the guy, "Hey guy? Do I got like grease on my face or something?" But he don't say nothin he's just starin at me like with his eyes all bugged out, seriously man eyes bugged out so fuckin far I could lick the fuckin contacts offa his eyeballs from where I'm standin.

> *He makes a licking motion.*

But I don't eh. I just keep talking and the guy keeps starin and I'm thinkin like hey freak what is your problem eh and then I sorta notice like he's kinda fixating on my lips eh and I ain't no dumbass so's I clue in pretty quick that this guy's hard of hearing and he's readin my lips so I start enunciating real carefully so's maybe he could understand better but it don't fuckin help eh he's just looking at me more eh and then,

Then it fuckin hits me right. Fuck my fuckin lipstick. Jesus I'd forgot eh cause I was workin in the back here alone and I wasn't expectin to see nobody right and now this guy probably thinks I'm the freak eh cuz shit man no doubt I got lipstick all smeared off and I even probably got it all over my teeth and I'm thinkin' classy Nicky real classy.

So I stop for a bit and crouch down to the side view mirror to reapply right. 'Cause I mean you gotta reapply eh, I don't care what they say about long last colourfast yadayada bullshit, they don't make lipstick that stays on in the back of a hot auto body shop eh. And believe you's me I know whereof I speak eh like I ain't no novice at this eh I been wearin this shit since like grade nine mech shop okay?

I figure it highlights my best feature eh. Like face it eh I got a mouth. What's that saying a mouth what could suck a golf ball through a garden hose. Yeah. I got that mouth. These lips could make women cry. So what the hell eh I advertise. Put on the lips score with the chicks eh. I mean face it right if I had been blessed with a monster cock or like a set of cans like Pamela Lee eh you could bet I'd be wearin clothing to highlight that area. But like my ol man says eh, Nicky you take what you got and you run with it eh. So *(kisses)* daddy I'm runnin.

So back to this yuppie fucker right. Now I've reapplied and I feel fresh and frisky no problem but the fuckin guy is still lookin at me with this disgusted look eh and now I know what the problem is eh. Fuck it, this guy obviously only has one problem and that is very simply, the colour! Which kinda pisses me off eh 'cause this ain't no spur of the moment Maybelline peach frost or candy apple shit. This shit is fuckin MAC!! And I know it is the exact right shade to highlight my complexion.

So I decide not to tell the guy it's the alternator belt. I tell him it's the fuckin alternator, and the fuckin clutch case and that he needs a new set of brake pads. The guy don't even flinch say's he'll be back Thursday and on the way out he stops, comes back and leans in real close to me eh and then he goes. "It's okay man… it's okay, I'm wearin ladies' underpants."

Jesus Fuckin Christ ladies' underpants!?! Ladies' UNDERPANTS!!! GET THE FUCK OUTA MY SHOP!

David Bateman

I Wanted To Be a Bisexual But My Father Wouldn't Let Me

My lover's hair was red
and his skin was pink
Even from a distance one could see
that his lips were chiselled, faceted
like those large, illustrated diamonds
in jewellery advertisements

His cock was not so different from his lips
It protruded, of course, slightly
perhaps two inches
if the weather was good

on the coldest day in winter
without the protection
of thermal underwear
it became almost vaginal
a very tiny love canal

during those times one might have imagined his testicles
as round floppy ears hanging slightly inward
along the edges of a small, flat, round-ish face
a one-eyed baby elephant even

when it could be seen
this flattish, knob-ish, round-ish, pseudo-appendage
was surprisingly well-formed
exquisite in fact

this beautiful little thing
this inverted cock
this baby panda's face
this pubic teddy
this inescapably unmarketable dildo…

When I had it in my mouth
or should I say
in that small space between my lips and my teeth
it would, inevitably, become
a struggle to keep a condom from

wriggling free
some flaccid length of latex
slithering along my gums

sucking his cock, needless to say, also meant, sucking his stomach.

I rationalized the entire experience each time I went down on him
three times a day on average
by telling myself that it was a
small beautiful doorknob
like the antique brass ones
on grandmother's house
that held ice, in winter
within beautifully designed crevasses
that attracted my tongue

a child's tongue sticks to an icy doorknob and bleeds
when it is removed too quickly
an adult's tongue, with proper precautions
and a certain degree of familiarity
say ten minutes tops
can lovingly and longingly
embrace a miniature penis
and make it something wonderful
something to call their own

sitting on it was another matter entirely…

splendid if not a little detached
because the end was so well formed
tailored, quite fat, and close to the body
it created what I fondly refer to as
the GI Joe effect

anyone who has ever rolled a condom over Joe's head
—circa late seventies—
once all the plastic heads had been replaced
by the fuzzy hair-like ones—
and inserted him
to the neck
into their anus
they will know precisely
what is meant by
the GI Joe effect

Bear with me those of you who have spent the better part of your lives sitting
on cocks the size of barstools…

Because GI Joe's neck
like the shaft of my former lover's penis
is so close to the body
and narrower than the head
the cock, once in, stays put

the angle at which
said penile object
must enter the sphincter, however, can
at first
be a disquieting, almost always
upright encounter

standing in fact, to insert
said small knob
into my hole
remains the only position
we ever managed to perfect

thus, the idea of kissing
while getting it up the ass
became a physical impossibility
holistic sex was a luxury
for my lover and I

smallness, to this degree
enables one to go down on the penis
and both balls
all at once

an astonishing sensation
the three graces indeed

since having known him
I have cultivated a tremendous fondness
for eating three grapes
cherries
almonds
cashews

and holding them in my mouth for minutes on end...

Granted, I have fetishized beyond reason
but what better use for fetishism
than the pursuit
of a little pink god
that the rest of the world would call
quite simply
dickless...

In a snug swimsuit, his cock, with balls
a still life of sorts
resembled three rather large fat knuckles

I would kiss his hips
and hold his little Easter basket (good Friday)
fondly and firmly
always trying to re-assure, never diminish

Someone once called it a large fat cyst.

We never invited him to dinner again.
A delightfully nasty sense of humour is one thing. Large fat cysts are another
matter entirely.

Salad Days

when I met Victor
I was what you might term
boyish

somewhat effeminate
in a soft porn sort of way

I asked him very early on
if I was like a little girl in his arms

an ageing little girl
but a little girl nonetheless

he said no
that I was not
that he was a man
who liked having sex with other men
and that I was on the
verge
of becoming a man

that's a very queer place to be you know
on the verge
you're there
and you're not really there
simultaneously
and something happens and you take the plunge
or you don't

and yes
our relationship
may have verged
on pedophilia in the very beginning

but hell!!!
it verged on a lot of things
but it never verged on love
it was always that—
located succinctly
within the vast territory of love
and it still is
and I just hope he makes it!!!
of course everyone thinks
he has you know what
I won't say it
I think we hear that little word enough
everyone thinks that he is in the hospital

because of you know what
well I can assure you
a man does not get up in the morning
after decathlon sex
give his he-wife
the sweetest kiss ever invented
then go to work and have such
a devastating attack of you know what
that he is rushed to the hospital

it was a heart attack for Christ's sake!
a good old fashioned heart attack

I think in fact that it is fair to say
at this point in time
that
you know what
is a disease
that forces people to sit down
in fact lie down
for a substantial period of time
before they actually croak

you do not do
what Victor did
just yesterday afternoon
clutch your chest in the middle of a board meeting
and fall over

heart disease is tricky that way

you can be rushing along a hall
walking
in fact
standing still
and it hits you

when you seemed fine for years
when your doctor the god
in a world where doctors are deities
and most doctors are men
and all those men
have to pretend
that they are constantly
exclusively
heterosexual
they have to pretend
that they never feel anything
and women have to pretend that
they always feel everything

but Victor was not like that!
he was not like that
he held me for twenty years
believing that he was not like that

and then one day
he has a heart attack
and one little piece of information
reveals it all

he is just another little god
another little deity
pretending

he was warned about cholesterol
he was careful
but he wanted a fun life
not just a long one

and if he doesn't make it through the night
and I cannot be there
because suddenly and shockingly
he does not want his lover of twenty years
at his bedside
because some of his executive friends
will see that he's a pansy

every one of them knows that he's
a god damn pansy
some of them just prefer to forego the floor show!

how could all of these years have passed
and I never once considered the possibility
of a very very very very very very
problematic death bed scene?

I mean, what does he think I'm gonna do?
turn up at the hospital in a little pillbox hat
and a pink Chanel suit
and wait for his head to explode?

I'm no fuckin' First Lady
but I'm not invisible either

so
I will just have to sit here
and wilt
and wait
and wait and wait and wait and wait and wait
until he can stand it not for another moment
and all the love that I give
will have to come from my heart
and all the love that I get
will have to come from
those boxed paper hearts in the basement

and if he dies
and someone puts his name
on the god damned
you know what
memorial

well fine

at this point in time we should all be there
no matter what we die of
we own it

we were blamed and blamed and blamed and blamed and blamed
and then one day
the whole world woke up
and took it as their own
but it's ours!
we own it!

we have worked so hard
and we will share
but we will not give our pain away
we will not dress it up
for the rest of the world
to feel comfortable in

it's ours!
we own it!!!
I am delirious
I am making no sense
whatsoever
it's all just flashing before my eyes

what on earth would I do without him!?

Student
Scenes

Michael Lewis MacLennan

Beat the Sunset

"Adam & Sacha"

Wearing latex gloves, SACHA sits on the edge of the bed applying lotion to ADAM's back.

ADAM   Your friend is sick in bed.

SACHA   You've been in a bed for four weeks now. You've probably lain there ever since you came home from the hospital.

ADAM   That's 'cause ever since I recovered from pneumonia, I got shingles. I'm in pain!

SACHA   And you could lie alone tonight in pain, or you could sit in a theatre with me tonight, in pain. The choice is yours.

ADAM   *(sarcastic)* Thank you.

SACHA   *(stops applying the lotion)* Look, I can't take away your pain, Adam. I'm doing what I think I can, trying to help.

ADAM   Why? Why do you bother? What the fuck are you doing here anyway? You say you're straight, you say you've no ulterior motives. You don't even know me. You wanna be in my will, is that it? There's nothing to give.

SACHA   I do know you, Adam.

ADAM   Oh, you've seen me a few times and you know me better than anybody.

SACHA   Yeah. I understand you more deeply than anybody does. I haven't known you since you moved, but I knew you when you were... becoming. An adult. Before this armour was up. You called me your best friend. You called me your brother – or do you want to forget that? We were a common front.

ADAM   That's a lark.

SACHA   What about our secrets, the plans we'd make together, our conspiracies, the books we were going to write together. I remember camping with you and sharing our fear of the darkness, shivering together... like... like...

ADAM   Like lovers.

SACHA   Sure, yeah, sure.

ADAM   We *were* lovers.

SACHA   We were not lovers.

ADAM   We were lovers, Mr. Denial, and if you can't admit that, then I don't know what you're doing here. It's not such a big thing. I'm sure your ample masculinity could deal with it.

SACHA   You call it what you want, and I'll call it what I want.

ADAM   It happened, and you want to forget it.

SACHA   My memory is just as valid as yours, Adam.

ADAM   Much more selective. *(tired)* Oh, Christ.

> *SACHA has turned to gingerly massage ADAM's neck.*

Mmm.

SACHA   How's this?

ADAM   Ahh, the smell of latex. Bastard.

SACHA   How's your mother?

ADAM   My mother? She's fine. She came by last Friday, for her visit. Short and sweet, kind of dull.

SACHA   Oh? *(ironic)* You must be getting along then?

ADAM   Naw, just tuning one another out. I'm not pushing her anymore. She can take her time.

SACHA   That's good.

ADAM   I'll be long gone and in the ground, but she can take her time.

SACHA   *(stops massaging)* That's a good attitude.

ADAM   You're not the one with the fatal disease.

SACHA   *(up, tearing the glove off his hand)* My life is just as fatal and uncertain as yours, Adam.

ADAM   Oh, don't get academic—

SACHA   The difference is, I'm living my life – what are you doing? Your attitude's driving you down, not the disease.

ADAM   What do you call this? *(as he strikes his own body)* And this? And this?! What do you call the bumps and blisters on my body?! *(throwing off mitts)* What do you call the hairy growths on my tongue, my wasting muscles, my poor, decrepit, aging body?! I watch it every day. I obsess at how it is disintegrating before my eyes. I'm aging a year every week, it feels, and at twenty-eight I'm an old man. I feel death happening, Sacha. I feel it in every pulse of my body, every bend of its creaking knees. *(now striking* SACHA*)* Every sweat-soaked night. I feel it, and it is terror. You don't. *(grabbing* SACHA's *neck)* So shut the fuck up.

> *SACHA fights back, pressing ADAM to the bed.*

SACHA   Okay, maybe I don't know what it's like. But I live with a constant fear that my brain is going to throw me to the ground for a short, quivering while. Suck out my breath and spit, my eyes blind and wide open, flicking air with my fingers…

> *As he says this, SACHA pantomimes a seizure on the bed.*

ADAM   Stop that. *(SACHA continues.)* Stop it, Sacha. Stop it!!

> *SACHA stops. Angry and disturbed, ADAM is up from the bed.*

Christ!

SACHA   But I get up every day. It's a part of me, I carry it, but it doesn't consume me. Sure, I have epilepsy, but I'm not stuck in bed all day.

ADAM   Good for you, Sacha – just go, this isn't working.

SACHA   Why? I'm not supporting your decline? No, I think it's normal to be afraid and angry, but I'm witnessing you in this, this… willed decline. You don't want to get better, and that's what I can't stand. You have chronic problems associated with HIV-disease. And you spend the whole time in bed wallowing in your sickness. Half your problems are because you don't look after yourself. You're self-fulfilling your destiny—

ADAM   I didn't create this diagnosis.

SACHA   No, but you're not fighting it! Yes, they say HIV leads to death, and you will die. They neglect to say that you might have a dozen years left, probably more. That would put you at forty, Adam. Have you planned for forty? You haven't even planned your next trip to the grocery store!

ADAM   Shut up, Sacha.

SACHA   I'm serious! Have you thought about *doing* anything? Volunteering? You're on disability now, so why don't you do something with your time?!

ADAM   Forget it. Christ, Sash, the worst thing in the world has happened to me. And I can't believe… I don't know how to function with this burden. Every morning as I begin to peel back sleep, this wave of dread and fear hits me like nausea. How can I get out of bed when every morning the knowledge cripples me? This disease has shattered everything I believed about myself. I wanted to show the world what a proud fag could do. And it's as if I got caught and somebody's saying, you fool, what were you thinking? It all seems like shrill hubris now. I come stumbling back home to care facilities and the hypocrisy of family. I don't know why. *(breaking)* She's right, I don't know what I want. AIDS is the worst thing...

SACHA   It's not the worst thing in the world, Adam. It's a disease, not a melodrama. Sorry, but it's not the worst. *(pause)* Adam, I...

> *They are close. SACHA holds ADAM's wrist and looks down.*

ADAM   What?

> *SACHA suddenly hugs ADAM, who winces in pain, then hugs back, strong.*

SACHA   Sorry. Sorry. I'm sorry.

ADAM   You're sorry. *(pause)* Your heart's just a-going pitter-pat. What's the message?

SACHA   I don't know...

> *ADAM leaves the embrace.*

ADAM   Are you horny?

SACHA   Uh – no.

ADAM   Well, I'm horny.

SACHA   *(unsettled)* Can't help you out on that one.

ADAM   Yes you could. Tina's not around these days, so you might as well get it where you can, while the getting's still relatively good.

SACHA   That's not my... thing.

ADAM   Just as well, you shouldn't touch sixty percent of my body anyway. By the way, I was lying about the blister on my dink – no problem with the mucous membranes. So. It's probably a shitty play. Most theatre here sucks.

SACHA   Oh, does it now. You suddenly an expert?

ADAM   *I've* lived in New York.

SACHA   Oh! Well! You *are* an expert. How can I offer an experience worthy of you?

ADAM   Don't know. But I'd need an aisle seat.

The Shooting Stage

Ivan & Elliot

> *Lunchtime, outside the school. ELLIOT eats his bagged lunch alone. He chews his healthy meal without pleasure. IVAN enters with his schoolbag. Silence.*

IVAN   Not that cold, is it.

ELLIOT   No.

IVAN   Thought I'd eat outside today.

ELLIOT   Free country.

IVAN   Look, sorry about that, uh, yesterday. Just joking around.

> *Silence. ELLIOT continues to eat. IVAN sits beside him. He periodically sniffs his fingers, hands and underarms, a nervous, ongoing habit.*

I know Derrick can be a bit of an asshole…

> *He pulls his lunch from his bag and begins to eat. White bread and a hard-boiled egg which he peels and devours.*

You tell your Dad?

ELLIOT   No.

IVAN   'Cause he'd tell mine.

ELLIOT   I know.

IVAN   Thing is, that's just the way Derrick is. You can't take it personal.

ELLIOT   You did it too, Ivan.

IVAN   We were just joking!

ELLIOT   You ripped my underwear.

IVAN   Me?!

ELLIOT   How do you think I explained that?

IVAN   Just throw them out! Geeze, Elliot, you know, if you just acted a bit less…

ELLIOT   What.

IVAN   The way you act, you set yourself up for this kind of thing.

ELLIOT   How do I "act."

IVAN   *(pause)* Like a girl.

ELLIOT   *(pause)* Well I'm not.

IVAN   Yeah well I'm sick of looking out for you. We're not in kindergarten anymore.

ELLIOT   I know.

IVAN   This ain't the old days. *(Silence. They chew.)* So you eat lunch by yourself?

ELLIOT   Most times.

IVAN   What happens when it's cold?

ELLIOT   I eat by my locker.

IVAN   You're not allowed.

ELLIOT   Well I do.

IVAN   Ooo, rebel.

ELLIOT   Fuck off.

IVAN   You fuck off. *(silence)* Doing anything this weekend?

> *ELLIOT shrugs.*

Hn. Thinking of seeing a movie on Friday.

ELLIOT   Hn.

IVAN   Wanna come?

ELLIOT   *(pause)* What movie?

IVAN   Dunno, but we could go downtown. My parents'll let me have the car.

ELLIOT   How'd you get that?

IVAN   Worked hard last weekend.

ELLIOT   Shovelling pig crap?

IVAN   *(beat)* Slaughtered a bunch.

ELLIOT   Huh.

IVAN   Yeah. They said I could take the car as long as I went with you.

ELLIOT   Cool. That's great. There's this spaghetti restaurant downtown? They don't I-D. We could have a drink after the movie. Beer.

IVAN   Sure.

ELLIOT   *(pause)* Just us, right?

IVAN   Maybe some other guys.

ELLIOT   I dunno…

IVAN   Come on, they'll be cool. You'd have fun.

ELLIOT   Truth is, I've actually already got plans for Friday.

IVAN   Oh right…

ELLIOT   I do!

IVAN   What.

ELLIOT   A show I'm going to.

IVAN   What, like a strip show?

ELLIOT   No!

IVAN   What then, "theatah"? *(pause)* Look, Elliot, I need you so I can get the car.

ELLIOT   *(beat)* Tell your parents you're going out with me. I'll say I'm going with you. We'll cover for one another.

IVAN   Right on. *(beat)* Was a good speech on swans.

ELLIOT   Thanks. We could go this weekend, see if she's back?

IVAN   Maybe. You'll tell your dad?

> *ELLIOT nods. IVAN nods and leaves. Eating, ELLIOT notices IVAN's bag, left behind. He considers it a moment, then opens it, looking within it. He stops a moment, intrigued. He pulls out a pale silk scarf. He picks it up, brings it to his face and inhales deeply. He pockets it, grabs the bag and dashes off.*

ELLIOT   Hey Ivan!

Jordan Patterson

Waiting for the Donald to Call, or Oprah, or Margaret Cho!
"Big White"

JOSE   So are we going to go or not?

JORDAN   I just don't know if I am going to be able to handle it. I just don't know if my mental heath is very good right now. The amount of crystal I would have to do right now to get in shape enough to take off my shirt at the parties would make my life turn into "The Truman Show." I am getting so paranoid.

JOSE   Well all you have to do is get some Xanax and then everything will be fine. That always helps; you can even talk at sketch parties now. Well and using less K would help.

JORDAN   Well it would be nice to see everyone. It has been a while.

JOSE   Well I think we should go.

JORDAN   How are we going to afford it? We owe Justin Lance like $600 bucks for drugs and I don't know if he is going to keep handing us drugs and saying its okay to keep putting it on the tab.

JOSE   He is fine with it. In fact he asked me if I wanted to sell up there so I can work off some of the debt.

JORDAN   But you know how much that sketches me out. I always think we are going to get arrested when we do that. Do you remember Pride in Toronto when we sold for him? I thought we were going to get arrested for God's sake. I wouldn't leave that party because I thought the police were going to be waiting outside for us. I sat in the corner at the Sunday night party doing bumps of K and chewing my nails. Every time someone looked at me my hand went right back in my mouth. I was fucking terrified. And you didn't help much. I asked you to sit with me for a while and you said the music was too good.

JOSE   We have already talked about that a million times. I was high too and the music was fucking great. I am a fucking dancer, what the fuck do you want me to do???

JORDAN   AH support your boyfriend.

JOSE   I tried; I always made sure someone was with you.

JORDAN   Yah you left me with that fucking bisexual couple. I thought the girl was nice until I realized her husband was in the back room of the party sucking guys off and she was actually hitting on me.

JOSE   That's not true. I made the Doyle's check in on you every five minutes.

Beyond Therapy

"If I Ain't Got You" by Alicia Keys plays in the background.
JOSE and JORDAN's apartment.

JORDAN   Hey baby!

JOSE   Hey.

JORDAN   What's wrong? I didn't bring you a burger honey, you said you wanted me to stop bringing unhealthy food home.

JOSE   It is not that. I was just watching an episode of "Oprah" and I just can't stop crying.

JORDAN   Oh I should have guessed.

JOSE   But this is different. I swear to God I just can't stop crying.

JORDAN   What's wrong baby? What was the show about?

JOSE   Lisa Ling was on; you know how she does that job now?

JORDAN   Yeah.

JOSE   Well she went to China. She was doing this expose on how Chinese baby girls are being killed there as we speak.

JORDAN   Baby, that has been going on for a long time.

JOSE   I know but they showed this clip of them going into this orphanage and there was a little girl called May Ming.

JORDAN   I heard about this.

JOSE   May Ming means no name in China. Can you imagine that? No name. Less than human. Nothing. There was a camera crew and they walked into this room and there was a girl chained to a bed. And she was crying but no tears where coming out because she had no hydration. She was trying to make sounds but nothing was coming out. Her lips were completely chapped. She was skeletal. She was two years old. She was left there to die.

JORDAN   Baby.

JOSE   No, don't hug me. I have to finish what I am saying. You never let me finish and I need to finish what I am saying. She is the girl who has been chosen to die this week. The orphanage picks one girl a week and they lock her in this room and leave her there to die. They don't feed her. They don't give her water. They don't go to even look at her. The other children are supposed to let the workers know when she has died. You could hear the cameramen saying that they had to help her. Then another person said no. They had to keep working on their documentary. He said that if they finished their project that they would have the ability to save more girls. That was the end of the footage. *(JOSE breaks down.)* I am not living like this one more second. I am not living in this relationship, in this apartment in this house until you and I decide we are changing. Right now, Jordan. I mean it. I will walk out that door right now unless you commit to me that we are changing our lives. You and I are going to change our lives.

JORDAN   Okay, I think that is an amazing idea.

JOSE   And when we change our lives we are going to China and adopting a baby girl.

Crumbling Beneath Your Feet

JOSE and JORDAN's apartment.

JORDAN   We have to stop arguing in front of our friends, it is getting way too embarrassing. Yesterday I noticed that the woman that moved in next door is spying on us. She has a one-year-old child and I think she is afraid of him being corrupted by our foulness.

JOSE   Would you want your one-year-old living beside us?? You have a foul mouth. And you always have. And so does your mother!

JORDAN   Is that really needed?

JOSE   What?

JORDAN   The comment about my mother!

JOSE   What comment?

JORDAN   I have a foul mouth and so does my mother!

JOSE   Did I say that? I don't think I said it!

JORDAN   It is exactly what you said. You said that I have a foul mouth just like my mother!

JOSE   Well, she has a foul mouth.

JORDAN   And I am proud of it actually. What seventy-year-old woman will tell someone to fuck off right to their face because they are pissing her off. That is a gift, not a bad thing.

JOSE   That is not a gift. See, this is the problem right here. You think that something like that is a gift. That your mother will tell the man working at the Super Value on Davie Street to fuck off is a good thing. It is not a good thing.

JORDAN   Your mother would do the exact same thing.

JOSE   My mother would do no such thing. My mother has an education and is smarter than just being a crass old woman.

JORDAN   What did you say about my mother???

JOSE   I didn't say anything about your mother.

The Worst is Yet to Come

JOSE   I just can't keep living like this. I always said this felt temporary. I love you but I can't be with you anymore.

JORDAN   What are you going to tell me, that it is not my fault, that it is yours.

JOSE   No this is your fault entirely.

JORDAN   Oh that is nice.

JOSE   But it is. I just can't take your negativity anymore. It's too hard, Jordan. Everything is so fucking negative. It is just not what I want in my life.

JORDAN   I know, I can't stand myself, Jose. Believe me, I want to be a different person.

JOSE   But you can't.

JORDAN   I would like to think that I can.

JOSE   But you can't. Everything that goes through your mind is negative. Every person you see you don't like. You find something wrong with everyone. Look at that asshole on the TV. Look at that loser, look at that fat girl, Jesus. Lose some weight.

JORDAN   I understand. I am trying to change. I am trying to change the way I look at things.

JOSE   But you can't. Jordan, I have been with you for eight years and you have always been the same. How many times can you get a chance to change, and you don't. How many times have you said let's try a fresh start. The fresh starts have run out. You're just not going to change.

JORDAN   Well that is pretty negative.

JOSE   I have to move on with my life. I am complacent with you. I am not moving forward. I can see myself with you in twenty years, fat and unhappy.

There is a whole fucking world out there and I want to start living in it. Not living in here, in this apartment, being unhappy.

JORDAN   And I want to start living mine as well, with you.

JOSE   But you won't, sweetheart. Every time you say no, I can't do that. Every time you say you can't be an agent again. Every time you make fun of someone or put me down. It takes away from me. You have to start living your own life by yourself.

JORDAN   But I love you so much.

JOSE   I know you do, but it just isn't enough. I love you too. If you don't change your life, you are going to be by yourself for the rest of it. Sweetheart, I really don't think anyone could be with you the way you are behaving right now.

The Deus Ex Machina – Dream or Not

OPRAH   Listen, Jordan, I have an idea. I know it is going to be kind of bizarre being that I am who I am. But I think that I could be your muse. When I read your play, the characters that you have created mesmerized me. You really write well for women. I feel that I have been a bit neglected by the film community. I honestly believe that you are the person I have been waiting to meet. I thought that it was Toni, but now I am not so sure. After reading *The Pitch* I just felt like we were really connected and that for some reason you and I would work well together.

JORDAN   Well Oprah, I can't even begin to tell you how flattered I am that you say that.

OPRAH   I just feel like you are connected to me somehow and that it would be stupid not to explore a working relationship together.

JORDAN   I think I know what you are saying, but I am not really sure? Are you asking me to work with you?

OPRAH   No – what I am saying is that I want you to work for me.

JORDAN   Of course.

OPRAH   I feel that some people think I am the Madonna of the talk show circuit. I am a one-trick gazelle. I would never say pony, have you looked at how thin I am lately?

JORDAN   You look amazing.

OPRAH   Do you have any idea how sick I am of hearing how amazing I look lately. If I hear how amazing I look one more time, I am seriously going to punch the first person I see.

JORDAN   I am sorry.

OPRAH   Oh God I am not going to punch you. It would be someone like the guy who said that I had plastic surgery in that absurd tabloid. The one who said that I was injecting things into my body.

JORDAN   I never read that about you.

OPRAH   Well I am sure you are aware that all of that stuff is absurd.

JORDAN   Of course I am.

OPRAH   It is just so stupid. I have a show on TV every day. When would I have time to go and have plastic surgery? I know I look good. But I still have a big ass and it ain't going to change unless I go under a knife and it ain't never gonna happen.

JORDAN   Good.

OPRAH   Do you have any idea how many people have approached me with a bunch of free cosmetic surgery ideas?

JORDAN   No.

OPRAH   Well you can imagine. I have seen myself a couple of years ago. I know how silly I looked in the past. But the thing that all those people who criticize me don't seem to get, is that I have the best life in the world. When I leave work at night I walk into my life. And no one really understands how damn good it is to be Oprah. Not one person other than myself knows what I did to be where I am now. And I love that. The only person that knows what I did to get where I am is me. And do you have any idea how amazing that feels? Do you want to know my one most important rule that I live by and what I believe has made me who I am today?

JORDAN   Of course.

OPRAH   Do you know what it is, Jordan?

JORDAN   What? For God's sake tell me, Oprah!

OPRAH   That I have not told anybody shit about my life. Everything that the public knows about me has come directly out of my mouth. You want to know something about me, ask me. But if you disrespect who I am as a person and the bullshit that I have put up with in my life, then you will get nothing from me. I will only tell people what they need to know about me. I hold the fact very close to my heart that I have far exceeded what my parents thought I was capable of. My parents didn't understand me, like you. I knew what I wanted from the day I was born and there wasn't anything that was going to get in my way. When I was a girl one of the very few things that I remember is a man disrespecting me. My first memory. A man trying to make me feel less than who I was. And I said to myself, that day, that I would never let anyone disrespect me

again in my life. You think I don't know what they say about me out there.
I know what they say. Controlling! I say IN CONTROL. Bossy, I say THE BOSS!
Who is in control? The one who is taking home so much fucking money that
I would not be able to spend it if I took Paris Hilton, Naomi Campbell, and
Goldie Hawn on a year-long shopping spree. I have so much money I can buy
myself an entire wardrobe from Louis Vuitton every single day for the rest of
my life. Clothes I will never ever wear because I don't have to. But I might like
the option so pick it up anyway! Do you understand me? I buy everything for
myself, for you, for your mother, for anyone I want to. Because I am worth it
to me. And I can sure as hell pay for it. In fact most of the shit I get is for free.
I will give it all away. All of it. I could live on the things people give me for free.
That's how lucky I am. Ya know why? Because I listened to my own voice. No
one else did. If I didn't step up to the plate I would have been sitting right
where your mother is. Think about that.

Jefferson Guzman

Playing in the Leaves

> *CAROL's apartment. JAMES on the couch watching "Bridget Jones's Diary." A knock at the door. JAMES pauses the movie, listens. Another knock. He moves to the door and opens it.*

GREG   Hey.

JAMES   Hi.

GREG   Is Carol here?

JAMES   Umm, no. She went to her mom's for the weekend.

GREG   Oh.

JAMES   She didn't tell you?

GREG.   No.

JAMES   Weird. She just left me a note. "Gone to Mom's. Water plants."

GREG   Oh.

JAMES   How did you get up? You didn't buzz.

GREG   I waited 'til someone came out.

JAMES   Kind of creepy don't you think?

GREG   Can I come in?

JAMES   Oh. Well, I was just watching a movie.

GREG   Oh.

JAMES   But I guess if you want to come in for a bit—

> *GREG walks right past JAMES and into the apartment.*

GREG   You don't mind?

JAMES   Well, for a bit—

GREG   I could go if you want?

JAMES   Hey, it's cool.

GREG   Thanks.

GREG sits on the couch. JAMES joins him. Awkward silence. They're both looking away. They slowly move their gaze to look at one another. They look away.

JAMES   Want something to drink?

GREG   You know, I should go.

JAMES   Oh.

GREG stands. JAMES stands. GREG moves to the door. JAMES follows.

GREG   Yeah. It's cool. Tell Carol I called.

JAMES   Yeah.

GREG opens the door and exits. JAMES locks the door behind him. He begins to move to the couch. There is a knock at the door. JAMES goes back and opens it.

GREG   What movie you watching?

JAMES   "Bridget Jones's Diary."

GREG   I've got some weed. Wanna smoke a joint?

*** *

CAROL's apartment. GREG and JAMES are stoned on the couch. The lights are low. Soft music plays in the background.

JAMES   Wait. You told her what?

GREG   I told her that I'm bi.

JAMES smiles, celebrating the fact that he knew all along.

JAMES   And... yeah, keep going...

GREG   I think what I'm trying to say is—yeah, that it's—I'm trying to figure out how much control I have over my life.

JAMES   I believe in fate. I mean if I could truly have control over my life, do you think I would have chosen to be gay?

GREG   You don't think you have control over that.

JAMES   No, really. Do you think I would have chosen something this hard if I could have done anything at all with my life? I mean, if you honestly think that I can choose to be gay, then why can't you sub-consciously choose to be miserable?

GREG   'Cause it doesn't make sense.

JAMES   But it makes sense to choose to be gay?

GREG   I don't know enough about it to really say.

JAMES   I don't know. I guess I just like to believe that everything happens for a reason.

GREG   What about coincidences?

JAMES   No such thing.

GREG   What about you and me? Bumping into each other at your work?

JAMES   Fate.

GREG   Okay. So what if it's not a black and white thing. What if it's grey.

JAMES   Huh?

GREG   Well, you didn't choose to be gay. I didn't choose to be bi…

JAMES   Okay.

GREG   But we do have control. I mean, we could choose to believe that being gay or being bi doesn't have to be hard or bad.

> *The statement has an affect on JAMES. GREG pulls out his rolling kit. He holds it up, offering to roll another joint. JAMES nods in approval but is still taking in the statement. He watches GREG start to roll a joint.*
>
> *Then slowly and softly JAMES puts his hand on GREG's. GREG looks up at him. They stare into each others eyes. JAMES puts his hand on GREG's face. He slowly traces along his jaw line, then his lips.*
>
> *GREG moves JAMES's hair off his forehead. The palm of his hand cups his cheek. His hand slides down his neck. Their faces move closer. They close their eyes. Their lips tentatively touch. Linger. They pull each other into a deep kiss.*

***

> *JAMES's bedroom. GREG and JAMES are in bed, they have just had sex. They lie beside each other but not touching, staring straight ahead.*

GREG   So you think I'm gay?

JAMES   I think it's a possibility.

GREG   I think I might be.

JAMES   Well, you could've just been curious but—

GREG   Oh?

JAMES   Well, yeah but—

GREG   Yeah. And now that I know what it's like to be with guys I can go back to women.

JAMES   Yeah.

> *Beat. GREG reaches over, begins to give JAMES a hand job.*

What are you doing?

GREG   Do you wanna do it again?

JAMES   I thought you were just curious.

GREG   I guess I still am.

JAMES   Look—

GREG   No, please don't make me think this whole thing through right now.

JAMES   Okay. But if not right now then when?

> *GREG kisses JAMES's neck.*

GREG   Later. After. I don't know.

JAMES   Look, I really want to but—

> *GREG notices that JAMES's eyebrows are shaped.*

GREG   Do you pluck your eyebrows?

JAMES   Okay. Pluck. You don't pluck a brow, you pluck a chicken. You tweeze a brow, with tweezers you know. And by the way, you don't dye hair, you're not killing it. You colour it.

GREG   So?

JAMES   Yes I do. But the hair is natural.

> *GREG moves closer to JAMES. Their arms touching. They start to play with each others' hands.*

GREG   What was your first boyfriend like?

JAMES   I don't know. He was just some guy. Why?

GREG   Just curious.

JAMES   That seems to be the thing with you.

GREG   Very funny.

JAMES   So?

GREG   What?

JAMES   What was your first girlfriend like? Did I know her? Did she go to our school?

GREG   No. Met her at a party. She went to that arts school. Carried around a plastic turtle everywhere she went.

JAMES   Like a purse?

GREG   No, she loved the turtle.

JAMES   And nobody ever said anything?

GREG   People would ask her why she did it.

JAMES   And she'd say what?

GREG   Why not.

> *They look at each other and share a small laugh. JAMES moves closer to GREG. He puts his head on his chest. After a beat, GREG puts his arm around JAMES.*

You sure you don't wanna do it again?

> *JAMES lifts his head and looks at GREG.*

JAMES   Why not.

> *JAMES kisses GREG.*

Salvatore Antonio

LOAD

LUC   I understand that you don't want to be here. Fine. But I did not need for you to fly in, just so you could spit vitriol and scowl at everything. You do not need to belittle our experience.

SIMON   Whose experience?

LUC   You were hanging out the window like some famished slut, collecting prizes at a county fair, or something. Look at yourself. This is not a joke.

SIMON   I'm giving them what they want. It's the same thing Papa used to do.

LUC   Excuse me?

SIMON   You heard me. When he and Mother would brawl. After he'd whip yet another brandy snifter at his study wall.

LUC   What are you talking about, Simon!

SIMON   It's all bullshit, Luc! Inside our house, everything was falling to shit, and outside he was doing pirouettes for the camera. I am doing exactly what he would have done in my position.

LUC   *(with a crazed, belittling laugh)* Are you really saying this!? Oh my, Simon. You don't possess a MODICUM of the class he had when dealing with his public. When dealing with anything, for that matter. All you're good at is prancing around like a useless little prince.

SIMON   You know what? Fuck this. I don't need to deal with this. You're a fucking psycho, bipolar asshole. I'm moving to another car, and you can go fuck yourself.

> *SIMON makes to move, but LUC fiercely intercepts him. He is desperate, almost manic. He blocks the way.*

LUC   No!

SIMON   If you know what's good for you, you will get out of my way.

LUC   You can't leave like this. Everyone will know our business. Please!

SIMON   Move, Luc!

LUC   Please, Simon!

SIMON   What is this behaviour, exactly? This is new. You realize you're having a breakdown, right?

LUC   What about *your* behaviour, Simon? This, *behaviour*, is this grieving for you?

SIMON   No Luc! No, this is not *grieving*. I am in no way grieving. I thought you understood. This whole thing is one big performance. It makes perfect sense that it be televised. It's fucking *entertainment*. Now let me go, or you'll regret it.

LUC   What are you going to do, Simon? Punch me? Actually make contact?

>   *Beat.*

>   *SIMON manoeuvers to grab LUC's face and kisses him forcefully on the mouth. LUC fights for a second, then stops in shock. SIMON registers that he has stopped resisting, and pulls away.*

>   *The two men look at each other in silence. SIMON is confused by LUC's reaction.*

>   *LUC has a spasm of pain and grabs at his stomach. He groans, and looks as if he is about to vomit.*

>   *He runs out, towards the washroom.*

>   *BLACKOUT.*

***

>   *Ten minutes later. SIMON stares into space. He is still unsteadied from the end of the last scene. After a couple of moments of inactivity, LUC reenters. He is shirtless and covered in sweat.*

LUC   You're still here.

SIMON   I was, um. *(referring to LUC's state)* Wow.

LUC   I'm vomiting, Simon. I'm vomiting now.

SIMON   Well, I'm about to start. Where's your shirt?

LUC   It's in the sink, dirty. Help me.

SIMON   What do you want me to do, Luc? I got you the pills and you flipped out. So how am I supposed to help you, tell me.

LUC   The pills are useless. They're not staying in me. First the diarrhea, now this. We're going to be arriving soon.

SIMON   I can ask Felicia to get a shirt from someone on the train. That's about it.

LUC   *(beat)* I can't do it.

SIMON Well, that's all I can do. Sorry.

LUC I can't do it.

SIMON What?

LUC I can't do the eulogy.

> *Pause.*

SIMON I'm sorry, what?

LUC You heard me.

SIMON Yeah, no.

LUC It's impossible. My insides are completely aggravated. I have no idea what's happening. I feel faint—

SIMON Well, sit. Luc—

LUC I'm having projectile bowel movements, all right?! I've never felt so sick.

> *SIMON says nothing. Pause.*

You have to read it, Simon.

> *SIMON laughs.*

SIMON Oh-ho, yeah. Right, Luc. You're serious, too. That's fucking hilarious!

LUC Simon…

SIMON That, is pure genius! No, I won't be reading fuck all.

LUC Language, Simon.

SIMON You must be really sick. Delusional, if you think I would. I'm sorry, that was a really pretty idea, but never.

LUC Simon, *je t'en prie.*

SIMON Ab-so-fucking-lutey not! *(beat)* God, wouldn't that be enjoyable. Force the black sheep to represent the family. It would be a final triumph for you and Papa, to watch me squirm.

LUC SIMON! THIS IS NOT ABOUT YOU! It's about our father, okay? Our father needs to be eulogized.

SIMON It's your fucking speech.

LUC So what? We share him; they're the same sentiments.

SIMON Excuse me? What world do you live in? We did not share him, and we sure as hell do not share the same sentiments. I'm sorry you're ill, Luc, but no. It won't work.

LUC Because you don't want it to.

SIMON   Absolutely.

LUC   You won't even try to consider—

SIMON   Don't you fucking talk to me about trying when it comes to that man. You have no idea.

LUC   Oh, here we go. No one has any idea how much poor Simon has suffered.

SIMON   I'm not doing this.

LUC   Come on Simon, it's another family funeral. It's another opportunity for you to make a scene, take a stand. Why wouldn't you jump at the chance.

SIMON   *(quietly, in shock)* You, are a disgusting person.

LUC   That's it? That's the best you can do? I heard that one last time, Simon. That's old. You used that one at the last funeral you hijacked, or did you forget?

SIMON   You and Papa "hijacked" that funeral, Luc. Blame yourselves. You used Daniel's funeral. Our brother's funeral, and you turned on me. I don't need to remind you. You need to live with what you did. I left all that shit behind. You had him all to yourself for three whole years, Luc. Now you bury him. I did it already.

LUC   You've spent the past three years stewing over one little thing. / One request was made of you and that was apparently enough to have you kill everyone off. "Oh, you're dead to me." "And you're dead too, because of whatever." Fine, Simon, one request you don't like, and we're all dead to you. You're such a powerful man, Simon. Enjoy it.

SIMON   / One little thing?

SIMON   A *request*? Is that what you and Papa wrote it off as? A simple request?

LUC   Our brother's funeral, Daniel's funeral was not the appropriate venue for you to have a "coming out" party, Simon. Papa had every right to ask you not to bring your man-friend.

SIMON   A "coming out" party?

LUC   Call it what you want. You ignored a very clear request. A reasonable request.

SIMON   My brother had just died in a fucking accident. I was not concerned with public opinion, Luc, forgive me.

LUC   It was not the venue for you to be parading around your lover, or partner, or / whatever. It was a solemn ceremony. And having him there would have distracted from the solemnity.

SIMON   / Boyfriend, Luc. / I had every right to have Mark there. He was giving me the support that I sure as hell was not getting from my fucking family. Understand?

LUC   You know you really are ungrateful.

SIMON   Really?

LUC   When Papa found out that you were a homosexual. When we all found out. Nobody berated you. Nobody attacked you. We all tried to be understanding.

SIMON   More like, mute. Almost as if you'd found out I had a terminal illness. I do recall a lack of eye contact and deafening silence, if we want to go back that far.

LUC   Papa was very forgiving, Simon. You can't deny that.

SIMON   "Forgiving"?

LUC   Not forgiving, I mean sympathetic.

SIMON   Whatever.

LUC   He simply asked that you not make it public knowledge. He asked you to keep it out of the press. He was being realistic about public perception, and whether you like it or not, his "public" is what insured our family's privilege and stability.

SIMON   Luc, I really don't want to listen—

LUC   Don't interrupt. We are Brassards. Papa made that name mean something. This nation loves us because we are Brassards. Our lives have been, and will continue to be far more privileged than most people's. He was trying to protect the image behind that name. He was actually trying to secure your future, Simon, try to understand that.

SIMON   Who are you talking to, exactly? Are you on speech mode?

LUC   I think it was a wise, and a fair request.

SIMON   Priorities, Luc. You think it's fair to ask me to pretend I'm not who I am, because who I am doesn't fit the image of the "family name"?

LUC   Simon, I'm trying to help you understand. Daniel's funeral was not the venue for you to be testing the boundaries of tolerance. Just like today, there were cameras everywhere, and reporters looking to sensationalize. Understand?

SIMON   I understand perfectly. If I'd had one of the fully reconstructed Westin daughters, snivelling beside me the whole time – *that* would have been appropriate. Celebrated, even. Instead, I was ostracized, and my boyfriend, my guest, was made to feel like a streetwalker, right before he was removed.

LUC   There was no need for you blow everything out of proportion. It was bad timing, during an unfortunate circumstance. That's all. Your little disclosure would have upstaged the real reason we were there. Which was supposed to be Daniel.

SIMON   Oh please! It had nothing to do with Daniel; your only concern was the fucking cameras. What was the real agenda, Luc? To uphold a sacred family experience, or, or… a political party convention? Hm? What exactly did I trespass on?

LUC   Your ingratitude is revolting, Simon.

SIMON   Answer the question, Luc.

LUC   He sacrificed everything for us, you little—

SIMON   Oh you're right, Luc. He did sacrifice everything. I think I finally get it, you know? I understand exactly what happened. *(beat)* Papa always told us that our family was here to serve the public, right? Right!?

LUC   Yes, Simon. Your point?

SIMON   My point is, he believed in that idea so much that he was willing to sacrifice everything for his fucking public. Including me. And what makes me ill, is that you find that noble.

> *LUC says nothing. His jaw tightens.*

But that's okay, because then I look at you, and I can see that he sacrificed you too. Only you can't see it. And what he did to Mother…

LUC   Don't speak for me.

SIMON   What do you have, Luc? Other than all the fake shit, all the empty benefits that come with our "name"? What do you have that's genuine, that's real? Hm? Who can you call at three a.m., when you're slumped in the corner of some hotel room and can't stop crying? Who the fuck can you call, Luc Brassard? The ambassador to China?

> *Pause.*

LUC   And what about you, Simon Brassard? What do you have, exactly? Yes, you broke free from us – congratulations. Yes, you're an independent man – a real trail-blazer. *(beat)* But can you honestly say that you're any happier than I am? Are you really free?

> *SIMON can't speak. Pause.*

What did I do to you?

SIMON   *(shaken)* When I saw that Mark was gone from his seat, I realized that Papa had actually had his people remove him from the church. I couldn't believe it. I ran to the main door and looked out, just in time to see him in the back of one of the cars, being driven away, as if he were some criminal. I remember how hot the tears were pouring down my face. I remember all the people looking at me, and realizing they had no idea of the cruelty of what had just happened. As I was stumbling back to my seat, Papa pulled me aside;

"Simon, I'm afraid you have miscalculated what your choices are in this family." *(beat)* I'm still trying to wrap my head around that one. And you, Luc, you were right beside him, like a carbon copy. You saw what had happened, and you stood by him.

LUC   Simon…

SIMON   Right then I probably needed you most. You were the only brother I had left. But you had jumped ship. You actually chose between him and me. Do you remember what you said to me, when we sat down for the service?

LUC   What good does it do to keep re-hashing all of this? It was a difficult day for all of us.

SIMON   I'm just curious, Luc, if you even remember what you said to me. Because I've never forgotten.

LUC   Simon, just let it go, for your own good, just—

SIMON   Yes! But do you remember? I was looking straight ahead, in shock probably. And you leaned in to me, and instead of comforting me or understanding, all you said was—

LUC   *(saddened and removed)* "Stop crying so much, Simon. People are watching."

SIMON   You remember. Good boy.

> *SIMON looks at him for a long time. He walks over to the casket and looks at it. He looks back at LUC.*

Good luck.

> *SIMON slowly makes his way to the door and leaves.*

> *LUC has another spasm of pain and crumbles to the ground. He cries in a fetal position.*

> *BLACKOUT.*

Julian Doucet

You Are Mine

The suite is typical of the sort you would find in a well-appointed hotel or club. The suite's bedroom, bathroom and lounge are furnished with the discreet and indifferent good taste of Waspish gentility.

RICHARD dressed in a suit, without a tie. He is again writing a speech.

RICHARD   On this sad day—

LUCY bursts in wearing a black cocktail dress just this side of tasteful.

LUCY   Not a word.

RICHARD looks up.

Not a fucking word.

RICHARD   We've been through this.

LUCY   Now she's sending me to a funeral in a cocktail dress.

RICHARD   A memorial.

LUCY   The difference being?

RICHARD   Dress code. They'll let anybody in.

LUCY   You're just like her.

RICHARD   Pin that tail on another donkey.

LUCY   It's insane to invite everyone to a wedding, and then try to serve them a memorial.

RICHARD   It's her day.

LUCY   You said that this morning.

RICHARD   The sun hasn't set.

LUCY   I can't do this sober.

RICHARD   Sober was this morning.

> *LUCY pours herself a drink. She has been drinking since this morning.*
> *She will continue to drink throughout the scene. She is not a drinker but*
> *stress is keeping her irritatingly sober.*

LUCY   This is what people do at funerals. Drink. To repress the pain.

RICHARD   You still have to feel it first.

LUCY   You think I don't have pain?

RICHARD   You didn't want them married in the first place.

LUCY   He was losing his mind.

RICHARD   He was misplacing it.

LUCY   Would you let me marry a man you knew was going crazy?

RICHARD   You married a potter. Define crazy.

LUCY   One of these days I'm going to stitch up that fork in your tongue.

RICHARD   My one beauty.

LUCY   What are you doing?

RICHARD   Granny asked me to scribble a few words for the service.

LUCY   You can't be serious.

RICHARD   I'm never serious.

LUCY   You barely knew the man.

RICHARD   Neither did his wives apparently. This hasn't exactly inspired them to speak on his behalf.

LUCY   Can you blame them? He died thinking of another woman.

RICHARD   He died thinking he was saving her from the Nazis.

LUCY   Some hero.

RICHARD   The man died. Someone should say something,

LUCY   Whitewash everything so we can all feel better about ourselves.

RICHARD   Time-honoured tradition.

LUCY   You're speaking for a man who cheated on his wife.

RICHARD   With her permission.

LUCY   You don't see something dysfunctional in that?

RICHARD   Dysfunction builds character. Puts hair on your chest.

LUCY   How can you find any of this funny?

RICHARD   It's cheaper than therapy.

LUCY   I will never understand why you choose to sublimate discomfort with humour. It must be a gay thing.

RICHARD   Definitely a "gay thing" I picked up from Granny. I hear it skips a generation.

LUCY   I didn't mean it like that.

RICHARD   They never do.

LUCY   I'm not like that.

RICHARD   Of course you're not.

LUCY   I was one of the first to march for racial and gender rights.

RICHARD   I was there, remember?

LUCY   I was trying to teach you that it's important to fight for a better world.

RICHARD   I was three. A better world was anything but a three-hour march singing "We Shall Overcome."

LUCY   You may not have been comfortable coming out to me, despite my every effort to the contrary, but I'm not going to pretend it didn't happen. We aren't going to repress. However much you might like to.

RICHARD   Very much like to.

LUCY   I am your mother and I'm not ashamed of my gay son. That's not the message I'm sending the world. I'm A-Okay with gay.

RICHARD   "A-Okay" with gay?

LUCY   Well how would you like me to say it? "Homosexual" is so clinical, "Queer's" too political. Polite euphemisms like "confirmed bachelor" sound prudish and repressed. Ridiculous euphemisms like "friend of Dorothy" sound ridiculous. Slang like "fag," "fruit" or "fairy" is completely offensive unless you're gay. Saying them if you're heterosexual is as bad as saying "nigger." Only I didn't just say "nigger." I mean I did, but I wasn't really saying it. I was using it as an example. To illustrate the politics of language. The re-appropriation of prejudicial language. I would never really say it. I mean I marched for Black rights, I—

RICHARD   Gay is fine, Mom.

LUCY   That's what I thought. It just seems the best, well the most, user-friendly.

RICHARD   That's what the new gay is all about.

LUCY   I wasn't trying to be flip.

RICHARD   The new gay is flip.

LUCY   I know it didn't happen the way you would have liked.

RICHARD   The way you would have liked.

LUCY   What's wrong with a mother wanting her son to be honest with her?

RICHARD   Not exactly the cornerstone of the parent-child relationship. You start with Santa and the Easter Bunny.

LUCY   Why are you avoiding this, Richard?

RICHARD   Until today, all of us were very comfortable avoiding this. Avoiding sharing your sex life with your family is a normal and healthy hang-up. How am I supposed to get through Thanksgiving knowing my grandmother's a polygamist and my mother's into light bondage?

LUCY   I just said that to—

RICHARD   That's between you and Dad.

LUCY   We're not really into—

RICHARD   Don't want to know.

LUCY   But even if we were—

RICHARD   *Really* don't want to know.

LUCY   Why are you so uncomfortable with this? Sexual freedom is at the foundation of the gay rights movement.

RICHARD   Hurrah.

LUCY   You're lucky you can be so glib about it.

RICHARD   You're lucky you can be so academic about it.

LUCY   Are you ashamed? Ashamed of being gay? Have I raised a self-loathing homosexual? I have haven't I? I can't believe it. I've raised a self-loathing homosexual.

RICHARD   You've seen our ads.

> *CLARA enters unseen by RICHARD and LUCY. She is still wearing her wedding dress, but now sports a smart, black veil. She is holding a tie.*

LUCY   Well it's not my fault. I made every effort. You were given every opportunity to grow into a happy homosexual. I did the research. I encouraged self-expression. I never made you feel bad for wanting to be a princess.

RICHARD   I was Superman the next year!

LUCY   Who is a muscle man in tights! You can't get any gayer!

Phae

The Wilds

HIPPOLITIS alone. PHAE and UNA enter unseen by HIPPOLITIS.
PHAE attempts to approach HIPPOLITIS but is stopped by UNA.
UNA indicates for PHAE to hide, she does so, then UNA approaches.

UNA   Ain't you a little old for the boy scouts?

HIPPOLITIS   What you doin here?

UNA   Your mama thought you could use a haircut.

HIPPOLITIS   She ain't my mama.

UNA   Step-mama. I came to talk to you.

HIPPOLITIS   No one comes to talk to me. I don talk. You wastin your time.

UNA   Maybe. But maybe you like what I has to say.

HIPPOLITIS   Leave me lone.

UNA   Gimme a chance… you gonna put some clothes on?

HIPPOLITIS   I ain't cold.

UNA   I don know how your daddy'll feel knowin you runnin round the woods with nothin but a scrap round your privates.

HIPPOLITIS   You can run faster.

UNA   You bein chased?

HIPPOLITIS   Why you here?

UNA   I have a message.

HIPPOLITIS   Phae want me home for chicken?

UNA   Not exactly.

HIPPOLITIS   What then?

UNA   What if I said I knew someone who thought… was wonderin…. You ever been to a dance?

HIPPOLITIS   …?

UNA   It's real nice. They do the gymnasium all up with decorations. Everyone dresses real smart.

HIPPOLITIS   I know what a dance is.

UNA   But you ain't never been have you? The boys all sportin matchin shavin cuts. The girls wearin too much eye makeup. Why is it that high school girls, who have the prettiest skin they ever gonna have, feel they gotta cover it up in whore paint I'll never know. Shit. I was the same at their age.

HIPPOLITIS ...

UNA I know no one never says how scary it is. Shit, we stole our courage from Daddy's bourbon. In the bathrooms we'd slide a bottle tween the stalls. You was so scared cause maybe you'd get caught or maybe after the dance your date'd take you up to Creeper's Hill an try to kiss you or touch you or maybe get inside you. You never knew if you wanted to or not. You never knew if the liquor wanted you to or not. But you was excited all the same. The music all loud and the bourbon warm in your belly. For a time you felt you fit.

HIPPOLITIS ...

UNA You ever wan go to a dance?

HIPPOLITIS ...

UNA You ever been asked?

HIPPOLITIS ...

UNA What if I knew someone who'd ask you?

HIPPOLITIS I don't go to dances. I don't go nowhere but here.

UNA When you gonna stop runnin round these woods playin cowboys an Injuns? What you runnin from? You scared of somethin? Bein loved maybe?

HIPPOLITIS I don need be loved.

UNA Bullshit. Everyone needs be loved. You jus never been loved right before.

HIPPOLITIS I don miss it.

UNA You never tried it darlin. Sweetheart, take it from me. One day your tits'll sag, your hair falls out, and you lyin alone in bed not cause you want to but cause no one'll have you. Ain't nobody wants that.

HIPPOLITIS I wan you out of my woods.

UNA Your woods?

HIPPOLITIS That's right.

UNA Last time I checked these parts didn't belong to nobody.

HIPPOLITIS I look after them and theyse look after me.

UNA Woods don look after folks. People look after folks. But then you wouldn't know bout that. Raised as you were. That's probably why you always playin at this Ranger Rick bullshit. You didn't get no proper love in the "formative years." A mama teaches her boy to love.

HIPPOLITIS   I had me a mama. I don need me another one.

UNA   How do you know? You never gave Phae no chance.

HIPPOLITIS   She ain't my mama.

UNA   You never let her. Head like yours all filled up with stories there ain't gonna be no room for a mama.

HIPPOLITIS   I had me a mama. I don need me another one.

UNA   All right then. Maybe you don need a mama. Maybe you need somethin sweeter.

HIPPOLITIS   I ain't gonna go to no fuckin dance. You wastin your time.

UNA   I know, I know that high school can seem all back asswards. You too mature for all that bullshit. Maybe what you need then is someone wiser, more experienced to show you what love be all about.

HIPPOLITIS   I don need be loved. I don need nobody. What I need is for you to leave me the fuck alone an get out of my woods.

UNA   You know what people say bout you?

HIPPOLITIS   I don care.

UNA   They say you don care for girls.

HIPPOLITIS   I don't.

UNA   But you from the same blood as your daddy. An you know how Big Daddy came by his name? Why there's a line of happy smiles an bruised thighs zig-zaggin cross the county.

HIPPOLITIS   You know who fuck like that? Rabbits. An rabbits is bout as low on the food chain as you gonna get. Why'd I'd wan to be like that? It's disgustin.

UNA   No it's normal. An normal boys wanna fuck girls. An if a normal boy had a chance to fuck a beautiful, more experienced woman, why he'd be writin *Penthouse* Forum—

HIPPOLITIS   *(interrupting)* Who'd wanna fuck you? Even an animal has more sense then that.

UNA   You think I wan fuck you? Don make me laugh. My pussy'd swallow you whole. I fuck men. Not queer lil boys who run round the woods like theyse Tarzan. You right. I is wastin my time. You cracked like your mama.

HIPPOLITIS   You take that back.

UNA   You know where it got your mama? Six fuckin feet under. You know where you gonna end up? In the nutter.

HIPPOLITIS   You say one more word bout my mama an I'll fuckin kill you you dumb cunt!

UNA   Now you sound jus like your daddy.

HIPPOLITUS   You shut up! You hear?! These my woods. You get the fuck out!

> *HIPPOLITIS exits. PHAE enters.*

Advanced
Scenes

David Roche & David Bateman

People Are Horrible Wherever You Go (Episode 2: Scotland)

> *Five performances at Buddies In Bad Times Theatre, Toronto; Sixteen at Solar Stage, North York; Two at Zeitgeist Theatre, New Orleans.*

> *Note: Following the success of the previous year's* People Are Horrible Wherever You Go, *a further episode was written, taking the characters to a new land. The play is four scenes, and has a running time of about 30 minutes. Scenes three and four follow.*

> *Time: The indefinite past.*

> *Setting: The hall of a vacant country mansion in Scotland, furnished with candelabras, an old gramophone and horn, and much dust. Spinster lady writers and companions ELVIRA and MAGDA arrived yesterday and set up camp, but were disturbed by the ghost of a playful young man, visible only to MAGDA, who has been left alone by a disbelieving ELVIRA.*

***

> *Darkness.*

MALE DICTATING VOICE   "The return of merchandise shipped as ordered has become a costly problem, and insofar as your letter of November 5 is concerned, we are asking your cooperation. These goods were delivered to you some months ago in exact conformity with your order. If they did not please you..." *(tape continues)*

> *Late afternoon. Lights up on MAGDA, seated by gramophone, mechanically writing in shorthand. The droning voice fades under MAGDA's inner thoughts. She looks longingly at a photograph of ELVIRA.*

MAGDA   I'll draw her near the brink, then stop, / And save her from the leap. / If for my pains she thanks me not, *(rises with pad, moving downstage)* if in remorse she fails to weep and clasp me whole, my body entering / In one raw, insatiate dance, then let her fall! / To hell! Her thoughts, notes, books and wit / To join her in some fiery pit...

ELVIRA enters laughing, flicking a towel at the air. MAGDA glances over.

(eyes back on steno pad, calm) You look ridiculous, you know, flicking a towel at nothing.

ELVIRA I'm not flicking a towel at nothing. I'm playing catch as catch can with a naked ghost.

MAGDA *(flipping over a page)* You're doing nothing of the sort.

ELVIRA And having a high old time of it. We've become companions, he and I.

MAGDA Rubbish.

ELVIRA T'isn't rubbish.

MAGDA You can't see him, only I can see him.

ELVIRA *(letting towel hang limp, facing MAGDA)* Why should you be the only one who can see him? Why can't I see him, too?

MAGDA *(weighs this, then)* I grant you that. It's possible that you can see him, too. But, not now.

ELVIRA Why not?

MAGDA *(simply)* He's not here. *(bursts into laughter)*

ELVIRA Has it not occurred to you, in your supreme arrogance, that though you cannot see him, others might?

MAGDA You mean the ghost has chosen...

ELVIRA To reveal himself to me, and not to you.

MAGDA *(scoffs)* Ohh!

ELVIRA He's changed allegiance.

MAGDA Just like that.

ELVIRA And what's more, he seems to prefer me to you.

MAGDA Prove it. *(ELVIRA considers.)* What is he doing now? *(ELVIRA looks about.)* Can you see him?

ELVIRA Frankly? Not at present. *(MAGDA looks satisfied, but quickly stiffens in alarm.)* Can you? *(MAGDA giggles nervously.)* Where is he now?

MAGDA *(reporting a physical contact)* Between. My. Legs. And I am being given the most delicious of caresses with that part of him he knows best to employ.

ELVIRA *(reaching for a glass of water, unimpressed)* And what part of him might that be? *(sips from glass)*

MAGDA His *(shudders)* breath. This blushing, freezing love. Sex as phantom androgyne, not one but both, not both but all.

ELVIRA   Indeed! Well, two can play at that. *(sits)*

MAGDA   This is no game, I assure you. *(MAGDA is now sprawled sideways in chair and speaks with effort.)* It is something rather more serious than that. Think of a question long asked to which there has been no reply. Think… of satisfaction felt in having that question answered. A thirst long endured, suddenly and most gratifyingly…

ELVIRA   Stop.

MAGDA   …slaked!

ELVIRA   *(puts glass down hard)* I said…

MAGDA   My naked, slay-ked…

ELVIRA   That's enough! *(rises)*

MAGDA   …thirst! Quenched – nay, drowned in…

ELVIRA   *(angry)* I have been a student of psychic phenomena for twenty years. I belong to the Society. Subscriptions to all their learned papers are in my name.

MAGDA   I thirst no longer.

ELVIRA   Why should the ghost appear to you, who never had time for my theories, never paid them the slightest attention, a scoffer… *(hits MAGDA's foot)*

MAGDA   *(gyrating to ghost's attentions)* I'm not scoffing now.

ELVIRA   An unbeliever.

MAGDA   *(fervent)* I believe!

ELVIRA   Infidel!

MAGDA   *(with increasing abandon)* Like a pony, *(MAGDA is upside down.)* like a swimmer! So lithe, ineffably agile. Boy-like but not; androgynous, urgent, discovering as it were, in the act, his need to bestow and possess. Inwardly, upwardly, pulsatingly, strivingly! Ending and unending. Now, together—

ELVIRA   *(fascinated despite herself, but snapping out of it)* Stop at once or I shall draw a pail of water from the well!

MAGDA   *(still feverish)* Water, what water? What for?

> *ELVIRA takes glass and dashes water in the face of MAGDA who stops at once, spell broken, her invisible partner fled. ELVIRA throws MAGDA a towel.*

(sputters, wipes water from face) You're jealous! No – covetous! *(a discovery)* You're jealous AND covetous!

ELVIRA   Why shouldn't I be, both! *(Sits. A beat, while they regain composure and establish eye contact.)*

(struggling for reasoned calm) This person, or spirit – whether imaginary or real, or occupying some spot on a continuum between the two—

MAGDA   "Doomed for a certain time to walk the earth..."

ELVIRA   —is patently someone, or something, at any rate, to which we both respond.

MAGDA   Who would've thought a young person of that sex could be so seemly...

ELVIRA   *(echoing MAGDA's tone, but on her own train of thought)* So comely...

MAGDA   So compelling...

ELVIRA   So insisting...

MAGDA   So enigmatic...

ELVIRA   So ecstatic...

MAGDA   So arresting...

ELVIRA   So ravishing...

MAGDA   So coy, and yet so forward?

ELVIRA   So firm—

MAGDA   —while yet so yielding. He is altogether a welter of contradictions, a sprightly sea fish, a dolphin. A porpoise at cross-purposes.

ELVIRA   He might as well be underwater, for all we can reach him. And he moves, as you say, like a swimmer.

MAGDA   Or an angel.

ELVIRA   Or a fairy.

MAGDA   Or a faun.

ELVIRA   *(urgent)* Or a demon. Are you a fool as well as ignorant? Blind to the dangers of the paranormal? The succubus and incubus! You could find yourself inhabited by the stalwart soul of a young colt, a human stallion. A boy stud.

MAGDA   My word... would I change...? *(touches her own sex parts)*

ELVIRA   No. You would remain a woman to the outward eye... but you would to all intents and purposes become UNSEXED.

MAGDA   Un—! D'you mean I should change as much as that? Walk with a swagger, my voice deepened? Adopt gestures of a proprietary nature, sweeping all before me in splendid, masterful possession?

ELVIRA   Any more than you already do at present? I should think so.

> *MAGDA already has the notion of letting the ghost inhabit not herself but ELVIRA, and thus restore ELVIRA's former dominant sexual style.*

MAGDA   *(secretly pleased)* But that would be alarming. To alter so radically, and virtually overnight. One can hardly see in it an advantage. *(to ELVIRA)* And you shouldn't like to lose me to this invasive power. Where would the old Magda be, the Magda you knew, the Magda you loved? The Magda—

ELVIRA   *(fondly)* —with a song in her heart? I don't know, where has she been all this time? *(brisk)* There's every possibility that the experience could leave you exhilarated, fascinated, and educated – in the ways of a superior lover. But I couldn't allow it.

MAGDA   *(smiling)* No. But I could. *(a chord of music)*

ELVIRA   Never allow the risk of – you could? You could what?

MAGDA   Allow *you* to risk the danger. *(A beat while ELVIRA registers this.)*

ELVIRA   *(an explosion of nervous laughter mixing embarrassment and hysteria)* No-o-o-!

MAGDA   Why not?

ELVIRA   Blessed-mother-of-Maude-Adams, me? Are you mad?

MAGDA   *(calm, but with purpose)* Come away in, then. *(moves to ELVIRA, who shrinks back to doorway)*

ELVIRA   But I still can't even see him!

MAGDA   *(advancing)* He'll see you well enough.

ELVIRA   *(retreating)* We can't predict what will—

MAGDA   You'll be safe.

ELVIRA   Magda, no. Better the devil you know than the devil… *(MAGDA embraces her.)*

MAGDA   I'm shutting the light. I'm putting you to bed in my arms. Rest.

ELVIRA   *(capitulating)* I mustn't. WE mustn't.

MAGDA   *(drawing her downward)* Go to bed, little father. The dark is light enough.

> *Blackout. A poetic kind of exorcism ensues, to appropriate sound effects, lighting and music.*

***

MAGDA   *(incanting)* Come Ghost. Good Ghost, Do thy utmost / Enter, mentor. Front and centre.

ELVIRA   I feel silly!

MAGDA   *(man's voice)* Put yer hand in my pocket; you'll feel nuts!

ELVIRA   *(alarmed)* Who said that? *(both look around for source of that voice)*

MAGDA   *(more incantation)* Thaw this mound of jellied aspic. Raise her to the heights priapic.

ELVIRA   *(ditto)* Sweet ghost. Dear Ghost. Here goes nothing / Raise me, rouse, give me fluffing! / In me place your faith and trust / Cause to stiffen what you must.

MAGDA   Come Ghost. Good Ghost. French toast. Bed Post. / Share your power twixt A and B, better known as M and E / Lip me. Dip me. Lave me. Choke me. / Quake me. Take me. Have me. Poke me.

ELVIRA   By this pillow, on this quilt / Vanquish fear and banish guilt. / Cause the bed to toss and tile, thrust your spirit to the hilt.

ELVIRA & MAGDA   Take the cake and leave the crust / round my middle round my bust / Legs astride or legs akimbo, be thou saint or be thou bimbo / Spawn of Satan, God or Limbo. *(music and effects achieve a climax)*

MAGDA   *(soft)* Is it over?

ELVIRA   *(ditto)* I believe so.

MAGDA   Was that him or you?

ELVIRA   D'you mean when—?

MAGDA   Yes.

ELVIRA   Impossible to conjecture. One can only state the facts.

MAGDA   This is not about facts!

ELVIRA   No.

MAGDA   Then—

ELVIRA   *(regular voice)* How do you feel?

MAGDA   *(ditto)* I? Wonderful! How do you—?

ELVIRA   Not bad. Capital, in fact, Just… capital. *(a moment of silence)* Penny! *("…for your thoughts!")*

MAGDA   What, for mine?

ELVIRA   Mmmm.

MAGDA   *(a beat, finds a box of chocolates)* Are you familiar with that clock in the town square, in old—

ELVIRA   *(finding cigarettes and lighter)* With little figures that come out on the hour? Yes. The Milkmaid and the Shepherdess.

MAGDA   At noon and six.

ELVIRA   And three and nine. Charming, what about them? *(lighting up)*

MAGDA   Don't you think they get awfully tired playing their roles, exactly the same way year after year? Always the shepherdess and always at three o'clock.... What if they should, you know, just for a change, come out at different hours? Trade parts. *(offers box to ELVIRA)* See what it's like to strike the bell from another angle. At noon and three, say...

ELVIRA   *(chooses chocolate)* Or six and nine. *(passes lit cigarette)*

MAGDA   You're beginning to get the picture. I'd say they're due for a change, those girls. *(inhales)*

ELVIRA   But not permanently.

MAGDA   *(reassuring)* No. *(exhales smoke)*

ELVIRA   They could go back to...

MAGDA   The old way, certainly, and then when that got tiresome, try the new.

ELVIRA   *(speculatively)* Noon and three... *(holds out box)*

MAGDA   *(trading cigarette for box)* Six, and nine. *(They eat and smoke. Unconcerned.)* Heavens, look at the time.

ELVIRA   *(ditto)* Time to go, I suppose. *(stubs out cigarette)* Pack up. Perambulate. Put "paid" to this whole damp experience.

MAGDA   Leave it, you mean? Like that? With no comforting moral, no explanation?

ELVIRA   *(as though dictating)* Since the Beginning, Woman has looked up and asked the eternal questions: What is Time? What is Life? What is Space? What is Death? Wise men tell us Death is only Alteration, that Time passes not, but describes a curve, and that both Yesterday and Today are with us always. The truth of what we...

MAGDA   *(silencing her with a gesture)* For those who believe, no explanation is necessary. For those who do not believe, no explanation... is possible. *(They embrace. Lights fade. Music up.)*

> *The end.*
>
> *In a choreographed curtain call, ELVIRA and MAGDA don Bo-Peep bonnets and play town clock figures shuffling on to strike the hour in turn. One carries a shepherd's crook and toy lamb, the other, a milkmaid's pail and stool. They bow and shuffle off.*

Sean Reycraft

Throat

> *Throat is based on the true story of LEO Mantha who, accused of the murder of Aaron "BUD" Jenkins, became the last man to be executed by hanging in British Columbia.*
>
> *In this scene, LEO has just entered the Bengal Room of the Empress Hotel – a bar notorious as a gay pickup joint in 50s Victoria. BUD is instantly drawn to LEO, and persuades Charlie (BUD's cousin and the Bengal Room's bartender) to set them up. Charlie accuses LEO of being an undercover policeman. When LEO protests, BUD demands proof – in the form of a convincing kiss. Charlie walks away, leaving the soon-to-be lovers alone...*

BUD   I picked the next song. What I hope is the next song. The jukebox's rented for the summer and it doesn't really work. Anything could be the next song. I like it. I get excited.

> *"Sincerely" by The Moonglows begins.*

THIS IS THE SONG! – the song I picked. You like this song?

LEO   I like this song.

BUD   Not everybody likes this song. My friend Jason—he's in the back—he *hates* this song. Jason likes songs like "Witch Doctor" and "Purple People Eater" and at Christmas? At Christmas he listens to The Chipmunks.

LEO   I've never heard of The Chipmunks.

BUD   Really.

LEO   I'm telling you true.

BUD   I'm liking you more.

LEO   You like me already?

BUD   After that kiss I almost loved you. You want to be alone?

LEO   You don't have to go.

BUD   I meant with me.

LEO   You meant with you.

BUD   Let's go.

LEO   You're taking me home?

BUD   I'm not taking you "home." My home's cabin 150 in Esquimalt – and as the Naval Captain tends to frown on me bringing dates "home," I'd have to say, "no." We're going to your home. Your house.

LEO   My apartment – my *sublet*, even I'm too embarrassed to see.

BUD   There's the parking lot.

LEO   There's police.

BUD   We could drive somewhere.

LEO   There's still police.

BUD   We could go upstairs.

LEO   Doesn't that cost money, "upstairs"?

BUD   You have money?

LEO   I do.

BUD   Then we're going upstairs.

LEO   You want to go now?

BUD   Not now. I want to wait.

LEO   You want another drink?

BUD   No more drinks. Just wait.

LEO   You said you wanted to go upstairs.

BUD   I did say I wanted to go upstairs.

LEO   Then why do you want to wait?

BUD   'Cause I wanna hear what the next song is. See, I didn't pick it – Jason did. He probably picked the "Purple People Eater." He does stuff like that. He does it to get me. Least that's what I think. You know what I think? I think you should do it.

LEO   Do what?

BUD   I think you should leave.

> *LEO turns away from BUD.*

I think you should go now through the hotel entrance, go up to the front desk and order a room. Maybe something big and high up – maybe overlooking the Parliament buildings. I like to look at the Parliament buildings.

LEO gets up from the bar, leaving a nickel on the counter. He starts to walk away from BUD—or from the world of the lounge—and toward the bed. He begins to undress, starting with his pants, and lets them drop casually to the floor.

I think you should take the elevator up to the twelfth floor, unlock the door and tie something special 'round the handle so I know which one to go in.

LEO finishes undressing and gets into bed to wait for BUD.

I think you should lay down, turn off the lights and I think you should wait for me. And oh yeah – I think you should leave me a nickel so I can order up one more song while you do that. I think you should go. I think you should go now. What do you think? *(turning to look at LEO)* You're smiling. I thought you'd be smiling. I thought that – I did.

***

BUD's standing holding LEO's pants.

BUD   *(entering)* I suggested you tie something special 'round the handle so I'd find you. You used your pants?

LEO   You should be more specific.

BUD   You should be more careful. Turn out the light.

LEO   I didn't think you were coming.

BUD   "Purple People Eater" wasn't Jason's only request. I also had to sit through "Jeepers Creepers" and "Yackety Yak" 'til they played my song. Are you gonna turn out the light?

LEO   What song?

BUD   "Dream." The light.

LEO   I want to see you.

BUD   I'm shy and demure. Turn it off.

LEO   No.

BUD   You don't get to do this—

LEO   I paid for the room.

BUD   I'm not some "commercial," Leo – some "boy" you hired up for the night. The light stays on? I stay dressed.

LEO   *(getting out of bed)* And I leave.

BUD   Sit down, Leo.

LEO   *(going for BUD)* Give me my pants—

BUD   Sit down.

LEO   *(tug-of-war now)* Gimme back my pants.

BUD   I want you to stay.

LEO   *(yanking hard)* GIVE THEM TO ME. *(BUD falls to the floor.)* Sorry – sorry I didn't mean – are you hurt? You're hurt.

BUD   I'm hurt.

LEO   I didn't mean—

BUD   I'M STILL HURT. I bit my tongue. Why would you make me bite my tongue? Sit down.

LEO   I'm sorry.

BUD   SIT DOWN. *(pulling out a large bottle)* Take it. Drink it. It's from Charlie. He's hoping we'll get too drunk to do anything. Every time Charlie sets me up he gives me liquor. Charlie gives me a lot of liquor. Charlie's a little conflicted. He appreciates the fact I got him the job, but then for Grandpa's sake I think he tries to "save" me. Grandpa's a Baptist minister who thinks I'm a speck of dust in the eye of the Lord. It's been a while since I've seen Grandpa. That's why I joined the Navy, you know.

LEO   You're a sailor?

BUD   You knew that. Esquimalt? Everybody downstairs is. This is us – doin' what sailors do. Like the song sings, "Everybody Loves a Sailor." Could you?

LEO   What?

BUD   'Nother drink?

LEO   I shouldn't have come up here.

BUD   You're not a sailor.

LEO   I should go.

BUD   I could've sworn you were a sailor.

LEO   I am.

BUD   For what ship?

LEO   For the merchant marine.

BUD   You're not a sailor.

LEO   I'm not?

BUD   You're somebody who works on a boat. You have to be with the Navy to be a sailor. I work in the paymaster's office, but I'm still a sailor.

LEO   I used to be a sailor.

BUD   Doesn't count.

LEO   But I used to be. I was a sailor 'til I made a pass at another sailor in San Francisco. He hit me so hard I woke up in a Navy hospital three days later. When I told the psychiatrist what happened I was told I had a "character weakness." I was a sailor with a "character weakness." I told them I didn't want to be a sailor no more.

BUD   See? You're not a sailor.

LEO   I'm leaving.

BUD   I had a naval psychiatrist tell me once I was highly effeminate and emotionally unstable. The "highly effeminate" bit shocked me TRULY and the "emotionally unstable" stuff made me really upset. Are you a homosexual of the feminine type? Or a heterosexual with fairly normal tastes who wishes to experiment in other ways?

LEO   What?

BUD   *(repeating)* Are you a homosexual of the—

LEO   Why are you asking me this?

BUD   I am a homosexual of the feminine kind. The sailors I suck off every other night? They're heterosexuals with fairly normal tastes who wish to experiment in other ways. I love psychiatrists. They're good at clarifying things. You want more to drink?

LEO   No.

BUD   *(taking off his shirt)* You still leaving?

LEO   You're getting undressed.

BUD   But are you still leaving.

LEO   I'll turn off the light.

BUD   Doesn't matter, Leo.

LEO   You don't mind?

BUD   It doesn't matter any more.

***

BUD   Jason? My friend I was telling you about last night who kept picking the crappy music. I embarrassed him once. I was too extravagant or flamboyant or or or weird and he was all upset about it. He gave me this article he's pulled from a magazine. I think it was American. But how could it have been

American? American magazines are all about movie stars. I don't remember anything about movie stars. All I remember is the list. The list of things homosexual men can do to help heterosexual people like them. I read it carefully. I memorized it well. One: Remain law-abiding. Be a good citizen. Set an example. Two: Don't think you're better than heterosexuals. If you think you're better than heterosexuals, don't show it 'cause no heterosexual will like you. Three: Don't flit, dress in women's clothing or make your voice swoop up and down like a seagull. Heterosexual people don't act that way, and neither should you. Four: Mingle. Don't be clique-ish. Get out and discover how nice heterosexuals can be. Five six and seven? – they don't really matter. Unless you want to hear them. Do you want to hear them?

LEO   No.

BUD   Eight: If a homosexual is in difficulty, don't play favourites. Straight people need help, too. Nine: Keep up with science. If they find a cure, use it – and FINALLY number ten: Avoid exaggerated cynicism (too late), self pity (too TOO late) and of course, super-romanticism and undue sentimentality (definitely TOO LATE).

LEO   I love you.

BUD   You weren't listening.

LEO   My Budsie-Wuzzie.

BUD   You really weren't listening.

LEO   I love you.

BUD   Leo there's people—

LEO   I love you.

BUD   —there's people around—

LEO   I love you.

BUD   —people like her.

WAITRESS   *(approaching)* Here you go, boys.

LEO   That was fast.

BUD   The food's not the only thing.

LEO   More coffee?

BUD   I'm fine. You fine, Leo?

LEO   I'm fine.

BUD   I think we're fine for now.

WAITRESS   *(walking away)* But do you think it's still raining?

BUD   I really don't know.

LEO   I'm not being "cynical." I *used* to be cynical when I was your age which is — what? Twenty-three? Twenty-four?

BUD   Twenty-two.

LEO   I'm thirty-one. I don't feel cynical anymore — I feel sad. And tired. But mostly sad. Which is different than "self-pity" which leaves — what did you say? "Super-romanticism and undue sentimentality?" Last night, when you asked me if I could love a sailor — nobody's ever asked me that before. Nobody's ever asked me if I could love anybody. I love you. I love you. I want to keep getting together like this — like that. Like we did last night. I don't know for how long — 'til one of us gets bored or unwanted or whatever else. All I know is that right now if you were to go away from me, life would seem very very long.

BUD   You believe that?

LEO   I do.

BUD   Then I guess I love you.

LEO   You don't have to say that.

BUD   But I should say that.

LEO   But you don't have to. Let's just say we're going to stay like this. Like we are. We can keep doing these things—eating breakfast, drinking drinks—renting rooms. Like this. But one thing.

BUD   What's that?

LEO   Only together. Nobody else. You. Me. Like this.

BUD   And you've done "this" before?

LEO   Yes. No. Yes.

BUD   You're giving me confidence.

LEO   I've done it before.

BUD   And how'd that work out.

LEO   It doesn't matter anymore.

BUD   Tell me how it worked out.

LEO   You're different than him.

BUD   I'm much better looking, aren't I?

LEO   I like you. I love you. That's all I have to say.

Blair Francey

The Splitting Effect

BABY   I'm sensing a problem.

WESLEY   ...Yeah.

BABY   Well?

WESLEY   I think... I think—

BABY   Don't be scared. It's me.

WESLEY   Exactly.

BABY   What? *Moi*?

WESLEY   Yes, but no—

BABY   Me. The problem.

WESLEY   You, me, us, and everything else.

BABY   You're gay. I'm gay. The issue is—

WESLEY   It's not so black and white.

BABY   Fine. Show me your shades of grey and I'll show mine.

WESLEY   I don't want this.

BABY   A tad contrary to what you were screaming out the other night.

WESLEY   Because all I wanted was sex! Why else does anyone go to those bathhouses? It was an escape. I didn't want to *feel* anything. I just wanted to get off with whoever would look at me.

BABY   Duh. I wasn't there to have a good night's sleep.

WESLEY   I'd kill for a good night's sleep in my own bed. I'm tired of escaping to the clubs and drugs, the music, the lights, the model bodies. It's all great fun at first, don't get me wrong, but I don't want to go home with complete strangers and wake up not knowing where the fuck I am or how I got there. I'm tired of running. It only leaves me wanting more – one temporary fix after another. The rush is over. I don't belong to that world.

BABY   Yes we do!

WESLEY   *I* don't. Me. It's not about you. This isn't about what I wear – it's only fucking clothes! I don't want to be defined by some fabricated label. Yeah. I'm... gay—fag, queer, homo—but it doesn't control *who* I am. You've had time to figure this all out. I haven't, but I need to on my own. I want to be me... whoever the fuck that is.

BABY   Sure. No problem. In the meantime we have two tickets to the Leather Ball—

WESLEY   LISTEN TO MY WORDS! I *need* to be *alone*.

BABY   Are you...?

   Pause.

   NO ONE BREAKS UP WITH ME!

WESLEY   Break up? What are we breaking up?

BABY   Our *relationship*?

WESLEY   What relationship?

BABY   Did I miss a memo?

WESLEY   There was no – we didn't have a relationship. We had, I don't know, something consisting of coffee houses, shopping, clubbing, drug abusing, late-night 24-hour pancake diners, sex – lots of that. But it wasn't a – you never asked me how I was. It was always about you. A relationship's a two-way street. We never had a conversation, and I don't mean one about celebrity gossip.

BABY   What about all the presents I bought you?

WESLEY   Doesn't automatically make us commonlaw. I don't even know your name.

BABY   Baby. Everyone calls me Baby. I'm your Baby!

WESLEY   I can't have a baby! I'm not ready—

BABY   Sweetie—

WESLEY   STOP CALLING ME THAT!

BABY   What would you have me call you then?

WESLEY   Wesley. Yes. My name is Wesley.

Edward Roy

The Golden Thug

"A Package Arrives"

Late afternoon. Lights come up on GENET sitting at the desk writing in the leopard notebook. The contents of GENET's suitcase have begun to spill into the room. There is a stack of fresh white paper on the desk along with other writing paraphernalia. There is the sound of someone knocking on the door.

GENET   Huh? Yes? Who is it?

PIERRE   *(offstage)* A package has arrived for you, Monsieur.

GENET   *(GENET continues to write without looking up from his notebook.)* Oh yes um… come in the door's open. *(PIERRE enters holding a large brown envelope.)* You said something arrived?

PIERRE   *(PIERRE holds up the envelope.)* Yeah.

GENET   *(GENET puts the notebook down and turns to PIERRE.)* Oh my dear I've been waiting for you.

PIERRE   Pardon? *(GENET snatches the package from PIERRE's hands.)*

GENET   I've had many lovers in my life, Pierre, but not one has ever compared to this.

PIERRE   What is it?

GENET   *(GENET rips open the envelope and removes his manuscript.)* My words.

PIERRE   Words?

GENET   Sometimes they shoot from me like streams of ejaculate.

PIERRE   Pardon?

GENET   Um?

PIERRE   Uh…. It's just that… you said words shoot out of you – like streams of…?

GENET   Like streams of cum. Yes. They do.

PIERRE   I don't get you.

GENET   You know what it's like when you're alone and absolutely certain no one will disturb you? Alone enough to stare into a mirror naked and truly give yourself over to that imaginary lover in your mind? Alone enough to ravage yourself? Know what that's like?

PIERRE   Uh huh…

GENET   And when you can no longer endure the self-torture of "delayed gratification" – when you're finally ready to…

PIERRE   Cum?

GENET   Yes. And cum and cum and—

PIERRE   Cum until you almost hurt yourself?

GENET   Yes! Sometimes that's how it feels when the words come.

PIERRE   You're a dirty old man.

GENET   Age has nothing to do with it. Words have always made me horny.

PIERRE   *(PIERRE laughs.)* So what's this thing that's making you so horny called?

GENET   *Prisoner of Love.*

PIERRE   Good title.

GENET   Glad you like it.

PIERRE   What's it about?

GENET   A man named Yassir Arafat asked me to write a book about the plight of his people. He wants the world to know about their struggle and suffering. He thought I could help.

PIERRE   Why you?

GENET   Because I'm for the underdog. The thief, whore, faggot, maggot! I am the Black American who wants equality, the Palestinian who wants his land back – the underdog incarnate who will always gnaw at the heels of my universal oppressor.

PIERRE   You hate Jews?

GENET   My dear boy, if the Jews were ejected from Israel today I would be championing their cause tomorrow.

PIERRE   That's just fucked. How can you think that way?

GENET   I'm French, it's in our genes. *(beat)* And soon I'll be finished my final draft and then…. It's in Gallimard's hands.

PIERRE   Gallimard?

GENET   My publisher. But that won't happen unless I get back to work, so if you'll excuse me. *(GENET begins to look over his manuscript.)*

PIERRE   Uh, Monsieur? *(GENET continues to focus on manuscript.)* What did you mean when you said you envied the intimacy of sweat?

GENET   Um?

PIERRE   That's what you said just before you fainted. You said something about liquid diamonds and envying the intimacy of sweat.

GENET   Did I? Mmm…. Liquid diamonds…. Liquid – A sparkling tributary…. Yes – yes – *(He picks up the notebook and begins writing in it.)* I remember – yes – A bead of sweat snakes down an angel's face like liquid diamonds. / A sparkling tributary—

PIERRE   / Yeah, that's it—

GENET   That frames the youth's divine perfection, this glorious stream that caresses the skin – I stand humbled…

PIERRE   Envying the intimacy of sweat.

GENET   It's good isn't it? I hope I can use it somewhere. *(GENET jots down a final note.)*

PIERRE   So what made you say it?

GENET   Oh I don't know um… psychic leakage? Freudian hot flash? Maybe a spark of recognition of qualities I once possessed but have now flown out of memory? Who knows what entices the muse to lift the veil? I'm just grateful when she deigns to bless me with her kiss.

PIERRE   So how many books have you written?

GENET   Five.

PIERRE   Only five?

GENET   Some people need to write a hundred books to get their point of view across. I only needed to write five. And then I started writing plays.

PIERRE   Oh, you write plays too?

GENET   They've been produced in Paris, London, Berlin. In fact one of my plays ran for four years in New York City. And a couple of them have been made into movies…. Not very good ones.

PIERRE   Yeah right.

GENET   Those idiot producers should have let me direct.

PIERRE   So how come I've never heard of you?

GENET   "For a long time I used to go to bed early." Do you know who wrote those words?

PIERRE   No.

GENET   Proust, ever heard of him? What about Rimbaud? Zola? Hegel?

PIERRE   Are those guys famous writers?

GENET   They were but apparently their clout is diminishing by the minute.

PIERRE   Do people read your books?

GENET   Do people still read?

PIERRE   Smart-ass.

GENET   *Merci*, I'll take that as a compliment.

PIERRE   Take it however you like.

GENET   I usually like to take it up the ass.

PIERRE   So you're queer uh?

GENET   Does that bother you?

PIERRE   Not as long as you don't get any funny ideas.

GENET   What a curse to lay on a writer.

PIERRE   You know what I mean.

GENET   *Mon cher* believe me, you could never compete with the erotic charge this gives me. *(clutching his manuscript)* Besides look at me, do I look strong enough to force you to do anything you don't want to do?

PIERRE   I guess not.

GENET   It was ever thus.

PIERRE   What?

GENET   Straight guys always feel less threatened around a faggot that's half-dead. No fear of being taken from behind when the beast hasn't got any strength left in its haunches. *(The light flickers.)* I hope your father remembers he's still got to fix that. Maybe you could do me a favour and go and remind him? *(GENET returns to his manuscript.)*

PIERRE   Sure, but it just seems kind of weird that you got your plays produced in those cities and into movies and whatever, and you end up having to stay in a hole like this.

GENET   This is a palace compared to some of the holes I've spent time in.

PIERRE   *(PIERRE moves to exit.)* I'll bet.

GENET   *(GENET looks up from his manuscript.)* Holes that stank with the sweat, shit, and piss of hundreds of naked men and boys who screamed at cold stone walls that were deaf to their misery. Walls that witnessed the flaying of loneliness until all that was left of the victims was a pitiless pulp.

PIERRE   Are you talking about prison?

GENET   Our shame gave us comfort when we were naked. Our farts filled the air with a sweeter fragrance than the flowers that held us captive.

PIERRE   You saying you were in prison? Bullshit.

GENET   Is it?

PIERRE   What did you do?

GENET   Wouldn't you like to know?

PIERRE   I don't really give a shit.

GENET   Of course not. I'm sure you have much better things to do.

"An Unexpected Interrogation"

PIERRE   You're fucking with me.

GENET   Oh really? I thought it was the other way around.

PIERRE   You must be losing it, old man, because I don't know what you're talking about.

GENET   I was asking about the kiss.

PIERRE   Kiss?

GENET   The guy you kissed. Was it Luc? Well? Was it? *(beat)* Ah, sweet silence…

PIERRE   How the fuck did you…?

GENET   I'm psychic.

PIERRE   You're full of shit.

GENET   Want me to prove it? Want me to tell you how your heart burns with desire when his quick temper shoots thunderbolts through it? How his wicked laugh fills it with joy? How his most casual gaze holds it; hanging by arteries transformed into vines, clinging to the overripe fruit that once pumped blood but now drips love.

PIERRE   You fucking faggot.

GENET   Have I looked too deeply into the locket of your heart, tough guy?

PIERRE   You don't know what the fuck you're talking about, you fucking pervert.

GENET You can shower me with spit if you like. But be warned, in that act of humiliation the strings of your venom will cascade through my being like warm honey.

PIERRE You're fucking nuts.

GENET Come on you can do better than that. *(PIERRE moves to exit.)* I see. Now the hasty retreat. Coward.

PIERRE Watch your mouth, old man.

GENET Or what? You'll finish me off? *(He grabs PIERRE.)* Go ahead. At this moment I can think of no better way to die than at the hands of an enraged beauty. If it was good enough for Pasolini, it's good enough for me. *(PIERRE frees himself from GENET's grip.)*

PIERRE I'm not a faggot.

GENET I don't give a shit what you think you are. I just know that you can't wait to feel Luc's warm lips devouring yours again.

PIERRE Stop it—

GENET His hot breath and hungry tongue—

PIERRE No—

GENET Then you hated it?

PIERRE No—

GENET You didn't hate it?

PIERRE I didn't feel anything.

GENET You felt everything.

PIERRE Why are you doing this, *hein*? Are you trying to drive me crazy? What do you want? *(PIERRE begins to unzip his pants.)* You want to suck my cock? Is that what it's going to take to shut you up?

GENET Put that away unless you intend to kill me with it. I can barely swallow spit without gagging. So who kissed who? Come on, you little closet case who kissed who?

PIERRE I'm not—

GENET WHO KISSED WHO?!

PIERRE Shhhh! – We were drunk…

GENET Do you get drunk together often?

PIERRE You going to jerk off over this when I leave?

GENET What do you care? So who initiated? Him? *(beat)*

PIERRE   Yes.

GENET   And you willingly complied? *(PIERRE nods.)* And then?

PIERRE   I don't remember.

GENET   Bullshit! That moment is etched on your lips, mind, and soul forever. You can try to convince yourself that it never happened but, like the murderer who has buried his dirty work in a far off desolate place, it'll come back to haunt you in your dreams.

PIERRE   No, I… I don't want to… I don't want to forget.

GENET   Why should you?

PIERRE   Because it's impossible…. It's…. For him it's in the moment, it's animal, he doesn't care if it's a guy or girl, he just wants to get off and…

GENET   For you it's something else?

PIERRE   I tried to convince myself that it was nothing. But then it happened again.

GENET   And again, and again, and again? *(PIERRE nods.)* Beyond kisses to full consummation?

PIERRE   I won't let him fuck me.

GENET   But you'd help him steal from your own family.

PIERRE   His family's cut him off, okay? And he's totally broke and—

GENET   You couldn't bear to see him suffer.

Short
Plays

Paul Dunn

The Bridesmaids' Conspiracy

> *Spotlight. MAN enters in a robe, and stands in spotlight.*

MAN   Good evening gentlemen. Oh, and ladies. I stand before you naked and ashamed. Well, not really naked. Naked under this. I was supposed to do this naked... a thematic thing, but it turns out I lack the courage. Big surprise. Funny 'cause that's what this is about really. Exposing yourself, despite the discomfort. I thought I was doing so well, you know? But it turns out I could do better. Could we bring in the bridesmaids, please?

> *Music. The BRIDESMAIDS—played by men, each holding a bouquet— enter and stand behind – their backs turned to the audience. Lights come up on the full stage.*

Meet Sheila, *(SHEILA turns.)* Tammy, *(TAMMY turns)* and Jenny. *(JENNY turns. The three wave.)* Maids of the bride. My cousin's bride. Friends of hers since kindergarten.

> *The BRIDESMAIDS giggle and strike a "Charlie's Angels" pose.*

They are quite a team. I got to know them over the course of my cousin's wedding. At the rehearsal, *(they laugh)* the ceremony, *(they cry)* the wedding photos, *(they pose)* in the limo, *(they squeeze together and talk excitedly and rapidly, all at the same time)* and FINALLY... *(they stop)* at the opening of the gifts. *(they glare at him, following him with their eyes during the following)*

I had never been to an "opening of the gifts" before. I thought it would be no big deal, I mean – it's the day after the wedding, the big part's over. We gather at the house, we're all hungover, and we mingle and drink... some more, while the bride opens her presents in the corner, or whatever, right? WRONG! It was a focused public display! You had to pay attention and look delighted! My cousin and the bride sat on folding chairs in the centre of the room, surrounded by the bridesmaids— *(they move into position)* Surrounded by everyone else. The gifts were opened in full view.

JENNY   A FRUIT BOWL AND OVEN MITTS! *(They clap.)*

MAN   The givers announced—

JENNY   FROM JEAN AND PATRICK! *(more clapping)*

MAN   And the contents duly recorded on a notepad, in order that the thank you cards would be accurate. Once each gift was opened, Sheila would take the card and pass it to the guest on her right, with the explanation that—

SHEILA   THE CARDS ARE BEING CIRCULATED.

MAN   The cards were being circulated around the room. So that everyone would get a chance to read them – what the hell? Is this a tradition? You mean, not only do I have to ohh and aww over the kitchenware being unwrapped, *(the MAIDS clap)* I NOW have to read every card!? You can't just give it a quick skim over and pass it on, either, eh? 'Cause the giver is WATCHING YOU! No, you have to examine it closely, smile warmly like you're touched by the picture of the little girl in the wedding dress and the frilly lace and the "May this day bring precious, precious memories and a life of joy and sharing and all your dreams come blah, blah, blah." God. I'm thinking, at least my card is simple. Tasteful. It's beautiful actually, 'cause all it is is a… is a… oh my God, IT HITS ME! Waiting in the pile of gifts is mine, a bed set, with MY card, with good wishes from me, AND MY BOYFRIEND.

MAIDS   WHAT!?

MAN   My boyfriend who wanted to send his love, who chipped in on the present. My boyfriend of three years who they've never met, or asked about. He had written how he couldn't wait to meet them, how they must come and visit us, how if my cousin's anything like me, he must be a catch… honey.

MAIDS   AWWW!

MAN   Now, my boyfriend couldn't make it to the wedding. Although a part of me wasn't altogether sure he was invited. Everyone in the family knows I'm a big mo, it's not that, it's that there is still a lingering… discomfort. And who knows how the other guests would feel about it.

TAMMY   Just so you know, I'm cool with it. I love the gays. LOVE THEM!

OTHER MAIDS   Shut up, Tammy!

> *TAMMY shuts up.*

MAN   Not wanting to make a fuss, not wanting to risk it, not wanting to look like I'm pushing my BIG GAY agenda; feeling like I'd caused enough trauma to my family just by being gay in the first place, and God, well I could give any number of excuses, right? The point is – my boyfriend did not come to the wedding. Nor did I mention him to anyone—

> *The MAIDS are shocked. He surveys them and turns back to the audience.*

But that of course is about to change. Once that card is opened and circulated, and read by all, someone's bound to ask who he is, the truth will come out, and who knows what awkwardness waits in store?

Little did I know. The bridesmaids had it all prepared. *(They whisper behind his back.)* You see, they were a team with a mission. A mission to make the bride's wedding as… comfortable as possible.

> *Music. The BRIDESMAIDS do a swirl—exciting jazz dance moves— around the man, ending in a huddle around a wedding card, frozen.*

When it happened it seemed to happen in a dream. The bride opens the card and reads it, and shows it to my cousin, who reads it and looks up at me as if to say…. "Did you have to?" Here I was, pushing that GAY AGENDA again. The bride smiles weakly at me. "Thank you," she says, and hands the card over to the bridesmaids. Here it comes, I think, moment of truth. But Jenny's usual announcement about whom the gift is from is delayed by a private conference—

> *They unfreeze, whispering.*

Instead, she just looks at me and says…

JENNY   Yeah, thank you.

TAMMY   What a "creative"… bed set.

MAN   While Sheila slips the card onto the pile of ones that have already circulated the room and come back to them. So that no one will see it. Then she winks at me, as if to say, don't worry about it, we've got it covered. Look how discreet and cool and on top of it we are.

> *The MAIDS giggle.*

And I let them. I let them hide my life from view for what I'm sure they had decided was everyone's comfort. Mine as well. How embarrassing it must be for me to be gay. Hadn't I been hiding it all weekend? Well, I'm not comfortable now. Nor should I be. In my perfect gay life, I would say "Hold on there, Sheila! No one's seen that card! Here, let me pass it around!" And then… and then… the room would have erupted in delight and curiosity, and I would say loudly and proudly, "HE'S MY BOYFRIEND and I LOVE HIM. HE'S SORRY HE COULDN'T BE HERE and I'M SORRIER. WE PICKED THAT BED SET OUT OURSELVES BECAUSE THE ONE ON THE REGISTRY WAS TACKY and IF WE EVER GET MARRIED YOU'RE ALL INVITED." There would have been oo's and ahhh's, and questions about my boyfriend, and why wasn't he here?, and admiring of the bed set by all for its taste and complimenting colours, answered with hilarious anecdotes about the two of us picking it out at The BAY of all places, THE BAY!!

> *The MAIDS laugh hysterically. Then stop abruptly and stare at him.*

But that wouldn't happen. The best I could have hoped for was silence, strange looks, as the controversial card was circulated. But in the end that would have been better than the undercover operation I had witnessed. We all may have been uncomfortable, but it would have been better.

> *He surveys himself.*

That's why I'm ashamed. I lack the courage. In my perfect gay world I would be doing this—

> *He opens his robe and flashes the MAIDS. One flees in horror. One faints. One stares in wonder. He covers up again and turns back to the audience. Back in a spotlight.*

Instead of this—

> *He snaps his fingers. Spotlight goes out.*
>
> *The end.*

Sky Gilbert

Theatre Manifesto

Dedicated to the memory of Paul Bettis.

Cast: MAN (at least forty years old), a beautiful YOUNG MAN.

SCENE: The MAN stands quietly beside the YOUNG MAN, who is lying on the floor with his eyes closed. Lights up.

MAN   Theatre is not like life at all; and yet it is.
Some violence is expected of all manifestoes; and yet Artaud did not mean blood.
In reality, this young man is not dead. He is an actor lying on the floor with his eyes closed—
probably in the vain hope of a fat paycheck, or simply to get his name in the papers. We all know that. Don't we?

> *Pause.*

Instead, I suggest, that he has died of AIDS.

> *Pause.*

There is only one way to bring him back to life.

> *Pause.*

Ironically, with a kiss.

> *The older MAN kneels down as if to kiss the YOUNG MAN.*

But will it work?

> *Pause.*

Oh, let's give it a try.

> *Very slowly, he bends over and kisses the YOUNG MAN on the lips; their bodies do not touch. They separate. A pause. Ten slow seconds. An eternity in the theatre. The old MAN sits quietly watching the dead YOUNG MAN. Then the YOUNG MAN moans. He stirs. He shakes his head a bit, as if he has been very long asleep.*

YOUNG MAN   I'm awake.

MAN   You're alive.

YOUNG MAN   I'm alive.

>   *Pause.*

MAN   All of us wish to know; what was it like to be dead?

>   *Pause, the YOUNG MAN thinks. Not artificially, but naturally.*

YOUNG MAN   *(firmly)* There is no right or wrong.

MAN   No?

YOUNG MAN   No.

>   *Pause.*

Can I be dead again?

MAN   *(fondly)* Yes.

>   *The boy curls up and goes to sleep, contentedly, quietly – no snoring, on his side, in a somewhat fetal position.*

Some violence is expected of all manifestoes; and yet Artaud did not mean blood.
Theatre is not like life at all.

>   *Pause.*

And yet it is.

>   *Fade to black.*

Index by Author

Index by Title

photo by David Hawe

Sky Gilbert is a writer, director, and drag queen extraordinaire. He was artistic director of Buddies in Bad Times Theatre (North America's largest gay and lesbian theatre) for 18 years. Since leaving Buddies in 1997 to pursue writing, he has published four novels, two books of poetry, four plays, and a memoir. He was recently the recipient of the Margo Bindhardt Award (from the Toronto Arts Foundation), and the ReLit Award (for his fourth novel *An English Gentlemen*). In 2007 ECW Press published his fifth novel, *Brother Dumb*. As his day job, Dr. Sky Gilbert holds the University Research Chair in Creative Writing and Theatre Studies at Guelph University.